Tena,
Your friendship
means so much to
me. I pray my
book touches your
heart!
Elizabeth

I Cried A River

The Journey from Tears to Triumph

ELIZABETH SHREVE

FOREWORD BY MIKE SHREVE

I Cried A River
The Journey from Tears to Triumph
Copyright © 2021 Elizabeth Shreve
ISBN: 978-1-949297-40-9
LCCN: 2021925124
Also available as an e-book

Unless otherwise noted, all Scripture quotations marked are taken from the NEW KING JAMES VERSION®. Copyright© 1982 by Thomas Nelson, Inc. Used by permission. All rights reserved.

Scripture quotations marked (ESV) are taken from THE HOLY BIBLE, ENGLISH STANDARD VERSION®, Copyright© 2001 by Crossway, a publishing ministry of Good News Publishers. Used by permission.

Scripture quotations marked (GW) are taken from GOD'S WORD® Copyright© 1995 by God's Word to the Nations. All rights reserved.

Scripture references marked (KJV) are from the KING JAMES VERSION, public domain.

Scripture quotations marked (MKJV) are taken from the MODERN KING JAMES VERSION Copyright© 1962—1998 by Jay P. Green, Sr. Used by permission of the copyright holder.

Scripture quotations marked (NIV) are taken from THE HOLY BIBLE, NEW INTERNATIONAL VERSION®. Copyright© 1973, 1978, 1984, 2011 by Biblica, Inc.™. Used by permission of Zondervan.

Address all personal correspondence to the author:
Elizabeth Shreve
P.O. Box 4260, Cleveland, Tennessee 37320
Office phone: 423-478-2843
Email: *elizshreve@gmail.com* • Website: www.shreveministries.org

Cover design and layout:
Michael McDonald
Email: *artfxdesigns@gmail.com*

Individuals and church groups may order books from Deeper Revelation Books directly. Retailers and wholesalers should order from our distributors. Refer to the Deeper Revelation Books website for distribution information, as well as an online catalog of all our books.

Published by:
Deeper Revelation Books
Revealing "the deep things of God" (1 Cor. 2:10)
P.O. Box 4260 • Cleveland, TN 37320 • Phone: 423-478-2843
Website: *www.deeperrevelationbooks.org*
Email: *info@deeperrevelationbooks.org*

Dedication

I dedicate this book to my one true love, Mike Shreve.

You came into my world and made the dry, dark places full of light and love. You're my existence. When God sent you into my life, you brought part of heaven with you just for me.

You are the most amazing husband, father, grandfather, minister, mentor, and friend.

Your word is your bond. Your kindness and loyalty amaze me. Your love of soul-winning is truly inspiring. You are my man! You never left my side during this time. You are a strong tower that I can feel safe in. Eternity with you will not be long enough.

Also, I dedicate this book to my children, Zion Seth, and Destiny, who are deeply loved. I fought to live for them. They are my joy, bringing such laughter to my life.

If or when they face things in life that produce tears, may the words of wisdom in this book guide them through to victory.

Lastly, I dedicate this book to those who struggle with sickness. I pray these words will cause you to fight harder, laugh more, hope for the best, and live longer.

Table of Contents

Foreword 9

Introduction 13

1. Tears of Shock 17

2. Tears of Fear 23

3. Tears of Sharing 33

4. Tears of Faith 45

5. Tears of Disappointment 57

6. Tears of Joy 67

7. Tears of Depression 77

8. Tears of Victory 91

9. Tears of Hope 103

10. Dry Your Tears 117

11. Epilogue / Things Cancer Taught Me 123

foreword

One of the most heart-gripping, yet motivating passages in the Bible is 1 Samuel 30:1-19 (and trust me, to get motivated, you have to read all the way through to verse 19).

It's the story of Ziklag.

It's the name of the location where David and his six hundred men were camped.

It's probably important to remember that they were a rag-tag, motley crew, who were rough-around-the-edges and beat up by life. The Bible describes them in unforgettable terms:

And everyone who was in distress, everyone who was in debt, and everyone who was discontented gathered to him [David]. So he became captain over them (1 Samuel 22:2).

The rejects. The outcasts. The scorned ones. Distressed. Indebted. Discontented. Smiles were probably at a premium in that camp. Laughter was rare. Peace was almost unknown. And worry was probably rampant (debtors who could not pay their debt off did not have a "bankruptcy" option during that era—instead, they were often enslaved or taken to jail).

Because they were all the object of Saul's scorn, every day involved tense strategies and new maneuvers aimed at outsmarting the enemy and avoiding capture (or more important than that, avoiding death). Then it happened. When they least expected it, tragedy struck. From a source they did not anticipate.

While David and his soldiers were away on a mission, the Amalekites attacked their base camp. All their wives and children were carried away captive and their encampment, utterly destroyed by fire. Everything. Gone. Ripped to pieces. Smoldering. And their loved ones—surely, they wondered if they would ever see them again.

Then David and the people who were with him lifted up their voices and wept, until they had no more power to weep (1 Samuel 30:4).

David was described as being "greatly distressed" (1 Samuel 30:6). Could it get any worse? It did.

David's men blamed him for the whole disaster and even spoke of stoning him. Then David made an incredible choice. I shake my head in amazement imagining what it would be like to feel as isolated as he did in that dire situation. The sixth verse goes on to say:

"David encouraged himself in the Lord his God."

I need to quote that again: *"David encouraged himself in the Lord his God."*

There was no encouragement to be found anywhere—except in Yahweh, the God of Abraham, the Maker of all things, the Highest Authority in the Universe.

Then David said to Abiathar the priest . . . "Please bring the ephod here to me" . . . So David inquired of the LORD, saying, "Shall I pursue this troop? Shall I overtake them?" And He answered him, "Pursue, for you shall surely overtake them and without fail recover all" (1 Samuel 30:7-8).

Miraculously, they did "recover all," just because God got in the equation (verse 19).

David wept until he had no more power to weep, but he dried his tears and pursued the promise. In a similar way, Elizabeth must have wept till there were no tears left—more than once. But she didn't stay there. She refused to drown in a pool of her own sorrow and disappointment. In her life-threatening battle, when everything seemed pitted against her, she too dared to "dry her tears" and "encourage herself in the Lord."

How do you do that?

- By setting your focus on God, and not on the problems

- By rehearsing in your heart His greatness, His power, His magnificence, and His invincibility

- By remembering what He has done in the past and daring to declare, "God, You can do it again!"

- By reminding yourself of God's character and His promises (who He is and what He has spoken—especially the living Word—the prophetic words you've received about your circumstance)

- Then by praising Him in faith-filled expectation concerning what you want Him to do—even against all odds.

David and his men recovered all.

You are about to read how Elizabeth recovered all. I pray that after you finish this book, you will remember this page and my final message to you, *"Tag! Your next in line for a miracle!"*

Mike Shreve
(Elizabeth's other half—so grateful she's still alive and by my side)

Introduction

I am a Cancer Survivor. I am a strong woman. I am a wife, mother, and friend. I am Cancer-Free. But my journey has not been an easy one. No one who has ever heard these words—"It is positive; you have cancer"—has ever smiled upon receiving this troubling diagnosis. This statement sent me down a long trail of tears. My whole life was turned upside down with just six words. My family's world was tossed like a ship on a stormy sea with these six words. How overpowering these six little sounds were to my heart and my mind.

My doctor—a gentle, loving, compassionate, and good man—was reluctant to tell me his findings. When his sense of responsibility drove him to speak, those words pierced my soul like fangs dripping with venom. I could feel the poison overtaking me within seconds. I have CANCER! I have what? Cancer. I . . .have . . . cancer. It just kept playing over and over like a broken record. Would I live? Would I die? How would I tell my children? The questions immediately began to swirl in my mind.

I am a Cancer Survivor. I am a strong woman. I am a wife, mother, and friend. I am Cancer-Free. Did it happen overnight? I wish. Did I stay strong the whole time? I wish. Did I escape fighting depression? Once again, I wish. Most of the negative feelings you can find in the dictionary you will experience personally following a cancer diagnosis. However, I knew I was going to have to get a clear head and control my raging emotions. I looked to God for help. Verses like Psalm 22:19 became even more important to me, "But be not thou far from me O Lord; O my strength, haste thee to help me" (KJV). And boy, did I need His help.

I am a Cancer Survivor. I am a strong woman. I am a wife, mother, and friend. I am Cancer-Free. This journey took me to places I never dreamt of going. But thankfully, during this journey, I had two great resources—God was with me, and my family was with me. I am so much stronger because of these two things. When I had no strength, God strengthened me. When tears would flow down my face, Mike would wipe them away. When I could not smile, Zion Seth would make me smile. When I felt all alone, Destiny Hope would crawl up beside me and loneliness would disappear. And my mother, who lived with us, was always there interceding. I knew that no matter what happened, I had a strong team that would never leave me nor forsake me.

I am a Cancer Survivor. I am a strong woman. I am a wife, mother, and friend. I am Cancer-Free. I have wanted to write this book for a long time. I have wanted to share my incredible journey. But every time I would start to write, I would get so emotional, I would feel compelled to quit. It has taken me awhile to be able to relive that battle without being overwhelmed again. It was the worst time in my life. But this battle helped me, too. It made me see what was really important in life: God, family, and friends. It made me realize that the God I have heard about my whole life really was a present help in time of trouble.

I pray that as you read this, you will get more than words. I pray you will be able to feel my heartbeat. I pray that your heart will beat with joy and hope in sync with mine. So, get comfortable, make a cup of tea, and walk with me down this long trail of tears. I promise, by the time we reach the last chapter, you will be strengthened in your faith, and we will be rejoicing together in the greatness of our God.

Tear Scriptures

Psalms 42:2-4

My soul thirsts for God, for the living God. When shall I come and appear before God? My tears have been my food day and night, while they continually say to me, "Where is your God?" When I remember these things, I pour out my soul within me . . .

Psalms 56:8

You number my wanderings; put my tears into Your bottle; are they not in Your book?

Psalms 126:5

Those who sow in tears shall reap in joy . . .

Tear Quotes

"There is a sacredness in tears. They are not the mark of weakness, but of power. They speak more eloquently than ten thousand tongues. They are the messengers of overwhelming grief, of deep contrition, and of unspeakable love." —Washington Irving

"Tears are only words that the heart can't express." —Anonymous

"It is such a secret place, the land of tears." —Antoine de Saint-Exupery

"The soul would have no rainbow, had the eyes no tears." —John Vance Cheney

Chapter 1

Tears of Shock

One day your life is normal (whatever your 'normal' may be). The next thing you know, you're diagnosed with breast cancer and suddenly you can't remember what normal was. I never really wanted to be normal until I did not have that option anymore. It was a day like any other day for me. I was rushing around trying to get my to-do list finished. Little did I know that day in October would change my life forever. On my to-do list were the words: Doctor's Appointment 1:30pm. I remember thinking, *I should cancel this; I have so many more important things to do.* My to-do list was about to become my "I-hope-I-can-do-it" list. Everything was about to change. Few things are as painful to the human mind as a great and sudden change for the worse. And boy, was I in for a great and sudden one!

It was supposed to be a routine checkup. I had skipped a year because it just didn't fit into my life. No big deal. I felt great. I was doing more than I ever had. There would be no sickness for me. After all, I am busy with the work of the Lord. I am invincible. I am woman; hear me roar. Mike was preaching in North Carolina. I was holding down the fort in Cleveland. I planned on rushing in and then rushing out and going on with my life. That day was different. We had known our doctor for twenty years. I trusted him. It was God and him that kept our babies alive during my pregnancies. He was with us at the birth of both Zion Seth and Destiny Hope. We laughed and joked as I walked into the office. Mike and I had no insurance, so I wrote my check and cut up with the girls in the front. I joked that he should pay me for what I was having to do. After all, do these kinds of doctors really think a smiley face taped to the ceiling will help you forget what is happening.

My name was called. Little did I realize that would be the last time for a while that I would hear my name over an intercom in a waiting room without almost passing out from fear. (When you're going through a trial like the one I was about to face, every detail is threatening. Hearing your name called out, wondering what is going to take place next, and hoping your heart doesn't stop during the conversation—these are the kinds of things you face. I was about to enter such a state of shock, my emotions would be raging at every appointment.)

The doctor and I went over the usual conversation. How are you? Where is Mike? How old are the kids? It was just a normal visit. Just like two old friends catching up with the times. Mine is in college. Oh, so is yours. It was light and fun. Then the atmosphere changed almost immediately.

I remember it like it was yesterday. The look on my doctor's face. The nurse shuffling her foot and looking the other way. He spoke haltingly, "There is something there. I can feel it. Can't you? Have you been doing self-examinations? I am going to send you for an emergency imaging."

The first words out of my mouth were, "No way. I am going home." His words pierced me (and still do), "Do you want to die? This could be serious. This needs to be checked." Emergency mammogram, why? Head to imaging! "You must go now. I'll call ahead. I want you to be seen immediately." The sound of concern in his voice was alarming. What is "imaging"? What is happening? Where am I going? What did the nurse say? It was like they were talking around me and my hearing was impaired.

My mind was barely processing what was happening. Where was I going? What was the next step? Who are these people? Why are they looking at me that way? I was ushered quickly into an imaging area. Having never had a mammogram before, I didn't know what to expect. The room was cold. The technician was young. There were strangers all around me. They must have known what I was there for. For one of the first times in my life, I felt completely vulnerable. Undressed and standing in front of a monstrous machine, my heart was pounding. The sound of the machine seemed eerily similar to the theme music to Jurassic Park. My whole body vibrated with the sound.

The young technician stepped behind her iron curtain. I could see her face. But what was worse, I heard her voice when she said, "Oh, my!" It was like she had a megaphone in my ear. Her "Oh, my!" echoed throughout the room. I tried to see what she was seeing. But my body was still attached to the machine. Unable to move, I questioned her, but she would not even look me in the eye as she matter-of-factly informed me, "The radiologist will send the results to your doctor. This is all just a process." Process? We are talking about my life. I wanted to scream – "Tell me!" I wanted to grab her by the shoulders and force her to tell me what she meant by the "Oh, my!" But instead, reluctantly . . . submissively . . . back to the doctor I went.

I've heard of shell shock. It is a term that describes things like involuntary shivering, crying, fearfulness, and even loss of memory. That sounds like exactly what I faced. I was in shock. I was a walking zombie. Just following the nurse, watching her mouth move but not hearing. "Sit here! Stand there! Lay down!"—were commands I followed almost mindlessly. It felt like I was caught up in a warped and threatening game of "Simon says."

My mind began racing with "What ifs?" I have always been a movie watcher. On the movie screen in my mind a movie started playing, starring me and all the things that *might* happen—surgery, chemotherapy, hair loss, death—all the harrowing experiences different movies and TV shows have depicted in heart-breaking detail. All of a sudden, every movie I had ever seen about death started playing. Julia

Roberts and Susan Sarandon in *Stepmom*. Would I need to make a quilt for Destiny? *Dying Young*, would I need to get a caregiver? *The Bucket List* with Morgan Freeman and Jack Nicholson. Do I even want to climb Mt. Everest? It was almost as if I could hear the theme song to *Love Story*. And the more frequently that 'movie in my head' repeated itself, the more difficult it became to think clearly.

Unfortunately, as soon as I heard the words, "You have Cancer," the ability to 'think clearly' became a bit difficult (to say the least). Equally true, and unfortunately, after hearing those words, thinking clearly became a matter of life and death.

Shock had overtaken me. Shock is defined as a reaction to the intensity of the bombardment and fighting that produces a sense of helplessness. It can manifest as fear, panic, flight, or an inability to reason, sleep, walk, or talk. As I sat alone across from his huge desk, my doctor explained to me what was going on. I could see his mouth moving, but I could not understand what he was saying. Had I gone deaf? What was that? He was telling me that I would need support, that I needed to make peace with my family and friends. Enjoy my holidays. That at the first of the year, I would need to use all my strength to win this battle. This is serious. How soon can Mike get home? I wanted to scream, "This can't be true!" I was numb. My doctor came around the desk and hugged me. Was this his way of saying goodbye? I said, "Will I live?" He hugged me tighter. As I left his office that day, it was as if I was in a dream. A bad dream (more like a nightmare). I don't remember a lot about my departure. I don't remember getting in my car. There was something in my hand; what's that? My check—the receptionist had given it back to me. On the seat next to me in the car there were

> Shock is defined as a reaction to the intensity of the bombardment and fighting that produces a sense of helplessness.

several pamphlets. All of them talking about the "C" word. As I slowly pulled myself back into a conscious state, I thought, *Where did those come from? How long have I been sitting here?*

Like Mike has often said, "There are two times to trust God: when things happen you don't expect and when things don't happen that you do expect." That sure applied to my situation. So, I suppose, in my heart of hearts, I decided my only choice was to trust God to take me through.

Overcoming Shock Scriptures

Psalms 143:3-9 (GW)

The enemy has pursued me. He has ground my life into the dirt. He has made me live in dark places like those who have died long ago.

That is why I begin to lose hope and my heart is in a state of shock.

I remember the days long ago. I reflect on all that you have done. I carefully consider what your hands have made.

I stretch out my hands to you in prayer. Like parched land, my soul thirsts for you. Selah

Answer me quickly, O LORD. My spirit is worn out. Do not hide your face from me, or I will be like those who go into the pit.

Let me hear about your mercy in the morning, because I trust you. Let me know the way that I should go, because I long for you.

Rescue me from my enemies, O LORD. I come to you for protection.

Overcoming Shock Quotes

"God has mercifully ordered that the human brain works slowly; first the blow, hours afterwards the bruise." —Walter de la Mare

"One type of shock is worse than challenges that are expected, and that is—unexpected problems for which a person fails to prepare." —Elizabeth Shreve

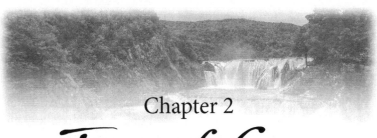

Chapter 2

Tears of fear

I know the scripture: "God has not given us a spirit of fear" (2 Timothy 1:7). I have quoted it all my life. So have most of you. That passage is imbedded in our minds, tattooed on some bodies, and forever in our spirits. But the truth is, fear gripped my soul. Let me give you another scripture: "Fear has torment" (1 John 4:18 MKJV). I was thrust suddenly and unexpectedly into the midst of a sea of torment. I was on an ocean of turmoil without sails and with no compass to guide me at that time. This raging sea had complete control of my existence. My mind swirled with negative thoughts like a whirlpool pulling me under.

I couldn't see any way out of this dilemma. I was in a perfect storm. My body, mind, soul and spirit were all lost in the wind and waves. It seemed like I could remember Jesus telling the winds and waves to calm down, but that seemed far in the past and I didn't feel Him in the present. I just felt the wind of fear and waves of anxiety. The wind was blowing my spirit around and the waves were soaking me. It seemed my faith was turning to doubt. Faith can move mountains, but doubt is what creates them.

It was a Friday afternoon when I heard those horrible words . . . the words that would haunt me for a long time. And to be honest, it still haunts me. Sitting in my car, I finally was able to shake myself. The fog began to lift. I called Mike. His words were strength to me: "We will get through this. We will overcome. I will make you carrot juice. God will not let us down during this time. We are more than conquerors." He was quoting and proclaiming. But I was doubting and crying. Yes, I should have been singing *Peace in the Midst of the Storm*. The only song I had in my mind was *You're Going to Miss This* by Trace Adkins. As the song echoed in my mind, I thought, *Yep, you're right Trace—I'm gonna miss being a mother to my two children and a wife to Mike—I'm gonna miss seeing their faces and talking with them every day—I'm gonna miss even the challenging draining parts of motherhood.*

Fear is a terrible thing. Your breathing speeds up. Your heart races. Your muscles tighten. You can't think straight. It consumes you. All you can think about is what you are facing. It is like a ravenous wolf chasing you. And you have nowhere to hide.

> Fear is a terrible thing. It is like a ravenous wolf chasing you. And you have nowhere to hide.

Fear can take many forms. Fear can hide and disguise itself. But sometimes fear just comes right out to defeat you. My every thought was plagued with fear: fear of death, fear of losing my hair, fear of the doctor, fear of everything. Fear is an emotional sin. Why would I say that? Because the Scripture declares that "whatever is not from faith is sin" (Romans 14:23). That's a tough one.

I had to shake myself loose from that emotion. Responsibility was knocking at my door. It was the night of Destiny's dance recital. I was the backstage mom. Of course, I was. I always jump in and help any way I can, hoping to use the talents God has given me to bless others. People, kids, parents, teachers, they were all depending on me. But I was broken. Broken in my spirit, broken in my mind, and now broken in my body. It was a strange feeling. I didn't feel sick. I didn't feel anything. I started quoting scriptures quickly, like: "I can do all things through Christ who strengthens me" (Philippians 4:13). "This is the day the Lord has made," I will "rejoice and be glad in it" (Psalms 118:24). It almost felt like a ritual more than a reality, but it seemed to work. It is actually immensely powerful thing to quote the Word of God even when it's difficult to force your mind to do it. The more I said it, the more I felt it.

Driving back to the rehearsal hall was one of the hardest things to do. Tears were streaming down my face. The phone was in my hand to call someone. But I didn't know who to call. Who do you drop that kind of bombshell on? My prayer warrior had recently passed away. I didn't want to be facing this. So why would I put someone else on this horrible ride with me. I was lost and alone. My pulse was throbbing. My mind was telling me, *This will be the last time you see Destiny dance.* All these precious children were there waiting on me. They were there for their holiday recital. Laughing, joking, tickling each other. Their whole lives were ahead of them. For a moment, I was envious of their innocence, youthfulness, and carefree attitude. Mine had been stripped away just a few hours before. All that was left were tears of fear.

I started helping everyone get dressed. Parents thought my tears were for their children. They were saying, "I know, I cry when I see them in the little tutus, too." Little did they know, I was crying for another reason.

Destiny's first dance was coming up. I went to the side stage to watch. The range of emotions were like a war going on inside of me. She looked at me and waved. Her smile was so beautiful. The Lord had promised me she would dance and sing. And here she was dancing like a prima ballerina. Or at least, trying. I could feel my heart breaking. I wondered if this was it. Would I be able to watch her dance again? What would she do if I wasn't there? Would Mike take her to dance? These questions fed into my fear. It was the fear of the unknown. The fear holds you back more than any other fear. Because with fear of the unknown, you don't know what you're pre-paring for or how to counter it. Fear of the unknown is like a room full of invisible monsters standing between you and any dream you have for the future. You feel the evil presence, but you have no idea how to overcome it.

How would I ever tell my little girl that I was dying? Would she remember me? Who would take care of her? When you are in the war of your life, the questions that your mind can ask are outrageous. It was probably a two-minute part in the dance, but in those two minutes, in my mind, I saw her graduate, marry, and have her first child. And this would all be without me. I felt a burning hatred in my body. I hated this disease. I hated that I had it. I hated that it was me and not someone else. But then that burning turned into love. Love for my husband, love for my children, and love for my call from God. I knew then, I would fight. I decided firmly, *I will not let this destroy my little family. I will not let it take my ordained and chosen destiny.*

Yes, I realized that I had this disease. But I also acknowledged in my spirit, it had no place, no hold, no power over me. I may have had fear, but fear did not have me. The stronghold had to be broken. Fear and me were fixin' to have a showdown. And it wouldn't be a knockout on my part. It would probably be a seven-round boxing match. Fear might win some, but I made up my mind, I was always going to get back up. I would never tap out. And eventually I would win.

> I may have had fear, but fear did not have me.

My first biopsy was scheduled Monday. Before arriving, I thought I would do some internet research. May I give you some advice? You should never YouTube medical procedures. I can't emphasize enough, stay away from WebMD. It's like opening Pandora's Box and releasing all kinds of negative reports.

As Mike and I sat across from the biopsy representative and surgeon, fear, anxiety, confusion—all these were whipping around us like a dust devil. I'll admit it. I was trembling like a bowl of Jell-O. Mike was a strong tower, of course. But I could read in his eyes, that he knew this wasn't going to be a walk in the park. My doctor started going over the procedure. Mike was listening like he was the one performing it. He was asking questions, getting clarification, and basically becoming a super surgeon in a matter of minutes. I wondered if he would ask for a white coat. I looked at him and for the first time in days, there was a smile. He looked like McDreamy from Grey's Anatomy. At least I would die knowing that I was married to him.

For once in my life, I was silent. Fear has a way of silencing you. I wanted to talk but there were no words. I wanted to ask questions but to me there would be no answers suitable for my ears. I did hear, not one but two biopsies. There was a new procedure. Great, I am a guinea pig. My head was hanging low, as only you can imagine. And if you can't imagine, I hope you never do. I am outgoing and forward. But for the first time in my life, I felt totally defeated. Maybe God was punishing me. Maybe I did this to myself. I should have just eaten like Mike. I could have learned to love greens and raw nuts. Maybe, I could blame my genetic line. But guilt, shame and blame have no place in this battlefield.

In a sweeping movement that shook both Mike and me, the doctor said, "Not in my house." His piercing eyes looked intensely into mine; his hand lifted my head and he spoke with authority right into my spirit. I felt that authority, I recognized it. It was not a doctor's authority. Hello! It was the Holy Spirit manifesting in a surgeon. It was almost as he transformed right before my eyes. One minute, he looked like a doctor in a white coat and then he transformed into a sanctified Optimus Prime. He informed us that he would return in a minute and left hurriedly. We sat alone in the room, wondering. We didn't look at each other. We were puzzled. In my confused state of mind, I thought maybe the doctor was mad at me. Maybe he could sense my lack of faith and he took it personally. And just maybe, the Holy Spirit in him was grieved with my unbelief.

The doctor returned in a few minutes. In his hand were printouts. "We are now going to read aloud together," he said. Truthfully, I was like, "Dude, I have cancer. Why in the world would I want to participate in some kind of read-along?" But then I looked down. The page was full of "faith" scriptures and "fear not" verses. He was a believer. He knew I needed to kick fear to the curb. I had to wipe my tears and say, "No!" to the swirl of negative thoughts surrounding me. I had to evict fear from my mind. I needed to shake myself free. You cannot face a battle like this with fear as your leader.

He explained that fear cannot walk with us in the biopsy room, and that he didn't allow fear in the surgery room. We had to also decide that fear had no place in our lives. We made the quality decision to read, believe, then declare those same verses under the power of the Holy Spirit until we felt a change in the atmosphere. We did that very thing. The more we read, the more real it became. Speaking it into the atmosphere was powerful. After about forty-five minutes, the surgeon said, "Now we are ready! Biopsy, here we come!"

Overcoming fear Scriptures

Deuteronomy 31:8

"And the LORD, He is the One who goes before you. He will be with you, He will not leave you nor forsake you; do not fear nor be dismayed."

When you're fearing a situation or an emotional challenge, when sickness, death, or pain unexpectedly show up, envision God saying this just to you, "I'm on your side. You are not alone. You are not forsaken."

No matter who leaves you after promising a forever-commitment, God will not follow that pattern. When friends, family members or co-workers disappoint you, He will never turn on you. When you get a negative report from the doctor, He'll never leave you. When others discourage you, He'll encourage you. Some of the lowest, most painful moments in my life have also been my closest times with the Lord. I'll never forget crying in fetal position on my living room floor after the diagnosis and feeling the presence of God's comfort and love like never before. It was so powerful that I found myself laughing through the tears, as Deuteronomy 31:8 burned in my heart. It was as if I heard my heavenly Father saying, "I am here. You will be okay. I'm all you need, and you're never going to be alone."

Romans 8:28

And we know that all things work together for good to those who love God, to those who are the called according to His purpose.

So much fear is based on the wrong assumption that when we have made a mess of a situation, it's too late for God's help. For the first few weeks, I beat myself up. Maybe I did something to cause this diagnosis. Maybe God was punishing me. What if He didn't love me? The thoughts were raging. But I'm living proof that God specializes in fixing mistakes. God has not only forgiven me after some blatantly unwise, selfish choices, but He's been quick to open doors, answer prayers, and pour out more blessings than I could ever deserve. He's so good. We combat fear by believing that He will turn our situation around for good, simply because He has a wonderful purpose for our lives. No amount of blunders can hinder the plan and purpose of God.

Isaiah 43:1

"Fear not, for I have redeemed you; I have called you by name, you are Mine."

God commands us not to fear or worry. The phrase "fear not" is used at least sixty-two times in the King James Version of the Bible. This is most likely because God knows the enemy uses fear to decrease our hope, stall our progress, and limit our victories. I've been a Christian for many years now, and I'm still in awe that God, who created the universe, cares about every detail of our lives. We belong to an all-powerful, all-knowing, victorious Father who cares deeply about us. When we really dwell on this truth, it's hard to remain fearful about the trials we face. By focusing on Him, and how He considers us His prized, redeemed ones, our focus naturally shifts from fear to faith. He redeemed us; He bought us with a purchase price; surely He will preserve us. Jesus Himself faced fear in Gethsemane and struggled against it, to the point of sweating blood, so He understands our plight. He's been there too! But whatever we're fearing—a bad diagnosis, family problems, financial struggle—just focus on the power of God, the One who calls you by name, and command fear to flee from your heart.

1 John 4:18

Perfect love casts out fear.

When meditating on this scripture, realize how God's love has made you less fearful of many things in life. It's so strengthening to realize that "God is love" (1 John 4:16). He is perfect love. The closer we come to Him, the less power fear will have over us. The more we feel *His* presence, the less we feel *its* presence. In His presence is fullness of joy, strength, comfort, and guidance.

This concept reminds me of times I've experienced "scary" situations, like hearing a strange noise in the middle of the night. I remember yelling for Mike, feeling terrified, but having total belief that whatever was happening, He would protect us. Or when I got lost on the road for what seemed like hours (but was probably only ten minutes away from my destination), I just knew Mike would do anything in his power to find me. When faced with even the deepest most crippling fears, we need to trust God with the confidence that a child has toward a loving parent. The key is abiding in that love, on a daily, even hourly basis. It has to be more than a biblical truth in our minds; it must take up residence in our hearts. We need to experience it continually—like the breath that flows in and out of our lungs.

Psalms 18:2

The LORD is my rock, and my fortress, and my deliverer.

Choosing a favorite psalm is like deciding on just one ice cream flavor, but this one sings the story of my life. Speak these words over the cause of your fear. God is our hiding place. For the Psalmist David, this meant sitting in a cave, fervently praying that trained warriors searching for him would pass by without discovering his secret place. For me, it was more like sitting in my car after a treatment, with worship music blasting, refusing fear, and praising instead. It absolutely works. We weren't saved and redeemed only to limp through life, riddled with fear and anxiety. God can only be our rock if we let him. Trust Him to deliver you from every fear that defies the truth—that not only declares His ability, but reveals His deep desire to deliver His precious ones.

Fear has no place in the heart or mind of a believer. Ask God to increase your trust and faith in His willingness and ability to deliver you completely from fear and anxiety. Ask for a deeper revelation of His love, then watch how powerfully He moves.

Overcoming Fear Quotes

"Courage is not the absence of fear, but rather the decision that something else is far more important than fear."
—Unknown

"I learned that courage was not the absence of fear, but the triumph over it. The brave man is not he who does not feel afraid, but he who conquers that fear."
—Nelson Mandela

"Each of us must confront our own fears, must come face to face with them. How we handle our fears will determine where we go with the rest of our lives. To experience adventure or to be limited by the fear of it." —Judy Blume

"Extreme fear can neither fight nor fly."
—William Shakespeare

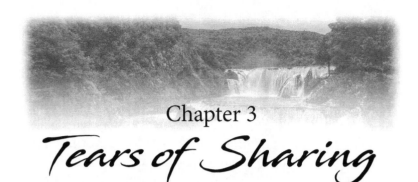

Chapter 3
Tears of Sharing

As children, we are taught to share. Share your toys, share your emotions, share your thoughts, and even share all your fears. It is usually healthy to share. But I was never good at sharing. My world was always *my* world. My things were always *my* things. My thoughts were generally kept under lock and key. Sharing was not for me. It was a trust issue. I didn't trust many people. This is something I still struggle with at times. Some of those I trusted in times past, well, they almost destroyed my faith in mankind. Truthfully, in my younger years, I lived a lonely existence. I could be in a room full of people but still feel alone. Everyone thought I was a party animal. But actually, I was like a turtle in a shell. I only came out of the shell when I needed to. It was only when I met Mike that I was able to trust again and begin to open up to others. He has always been my confidante, my person, my reason. My trust level was built up through his influence.

One of the first things they tell you when you are diagnosed with a life-threatening disease is to get a strong support system. I chuckled when the advisor told me that. My support system consisted of M & M (not the candy). It was Mike and Mother. Even telling them was hard. I called Mike from the doctor's office. My doctor insisted. There was the usual, "Hello, honey. I love you, honey. See you soon, honey." And then, the ax hit the tree. "Mike, I am at the doctor's office." Little did my wonderful man know the size of the tree that was about to fall around us. The doctor had screamed "Timber" in my ear. "Honey, I am sick. I have . . . " For the first little while, the word "cancer" is so overpowering, my mind would not allow me to say it out loud. It was on the tip of my tongue, but I just could not bear to speak it. The silence from the other end was petrifying. I knew that he was shaken. The word "cancer" can strike a chord of anxiety in even the strongest Christian. For Mike, that was saying a lot. I was waiting for something. Say something. Anything. But sometimes, there are just no words that can be spoken. We sat in silence. He was in North Carolina preaching and I was alone in my car in Tennessee. Are you sure? Are they sure? How do you know? How do they know? So many questions and so few answers. I stumbled over my own words as I tried to tell him the progression of what had happened during the appointment: "annual checkup . . . results . . . healthy . . . wait . . . there's a lump . . . quick, go to imaging . . . huge tumor… and then cancer."

But then, my spiritual warrior and my dearest friend pushed his way through the fog of that halting description. Words of power began to flow from him, words of deliverance, and words of strength. I could feel it. It was electrifying coming through the phone line. I tried to hold on to that hope as much as I could. I wish I could tell you that I didn't fall back into doubt. I wish there were no times of fear. But cancer is a journey. It is a process of ups and downs. It is a continual fight. And at that moment, the doctor's words and scans were winning against Mike's encouragement.

> One of the hardest things about learning you have a life-threatening or terminal illness is figuring out how to tell the people you love.

One of the hardest things about learning you have a life-threatening or terminal illness is figuring out how to tell the people you love. How do you tell people that you are sick? How do you tell them you might die? How do you say, "Goodbye" when you are living? Even now, I hear people whisper the word "cancer." I never wanted pity. I didn't want to be seen as a victim. However, I didn't want people to say it out loud. So, my sharing was with very few.

I am a big social media person. But I never shared it on any social sites. It was a private and personal struggle for me. Should I have shared more? Who knows? It was just the way I chose to do it. My advocate was always pushing me to be more open. I am not an open person. She always lost when we discussed this issue. You can't predict how family members or other loved ones will react. Some will cry. Some will just act numb. Some will be eager to jump in and be the rush-to-the-rescue person. I didn't need or want any of those things. I really just wanted to be left alone. This is probably not the right thing to do. But it is the response that I chose. I have found that each person who walks this road does so in a different way. Some people get everyone involved. Others would prefer to have no one involved. It needs to be up to the individual. Sometimes that is hard, but we need to be respectful of each person's decision.

I had children; I knew sharing the news with them was going to be a delicate and potentially stressful conversation. While I didn't want to unnecessarily frighten them, I knew it was important to let them know. Zion Seth didn't take the news well. It was heartbreaking to watch him break down and cry. We sat on the bed, holding each other and simply crying together. I don't know which one of us was hurting the most. I prayed and asked God to show me how to help him settle this in his mind. Since he was so intellectual, I felt like it was right to discuss the specifics with him. I took him to the treatment facility. He met the oncologist, radiologist, nurse practitioners, and surgeon. He went into the radiation room. This was calming to him. He was able to process the treatments and surgery in his mind.

Destiny was a whole new ballgame. She was ten years younger than Zion Seth. Her life consisted of Barbies, ballet, and Dora the Explorer. Her face was always a picture-perfect expression of innocence and purity. How could I possibly take that away from her? How do you look at a small child and explain cancer? How do you explain the possibility of death? At this point in her life, she had never lost anyone or anything dear to her. She didn't know fear—except fear of the dark and fear of the neighbor's dog. I dreaded talking to her about what was about to transpire. If you remember, I was diagnosed on the day of her winter dance recital.

We had been trying to do life as usual. We were holding it together as best we could. The holidays were upon us. Trees were up. We had a Christmas Disney trip planned that had to be cancelled. I took this as a good time to explain to her why we would not be going on our trip. I sat her down, told her that Mommy was going to be seeing some doctors. I explained that everything would be okay. There was something in my body that had to be removed. It would take a little time. My words were soothing and calming. I knew I was doing a really good job at this conversation. I even thought, *I should write a book about how to do this.* Then, I said we would not be going to Disney that year. She started crying so hard. I was comforting her. I was trying to convince her it would be fine. Mommy would be good. The doctors are going to fix me. God is going to heal me. Life was not over. As a mother, I was pouring every ounce of reassurance I could find into my sweet little girl. Crocodile tears running down her face. She stopped crying and looked at me so sincerely, she said, "I'm not crying because of you! I'm crying because we aren't going to Disney."

Thank God for pure, childhood innocence and honesty!

One day, I finally decided to tell my best friend, Vicki. There we were, sitting in her office. She was doing so well with the news. We were joking and laughing. I said, "I will finally be skinny." We were trying to look at the positive side. She is my go-to person. I thought, *Okay, maybe, just maybe I can share with others.* Support is all I had been hearing for weeks. People will be a strength to you. I looked at her, and simply said, "Let's enjoy Thanksgiving and Christmas together. It could be my last." Oh no, Niagara Falls hit her. She never cries. What is she doing, crying? I had no idea what to do with that. Stop the crying. I am going to cry. I ended up consoling her. We both cried a little. Then we started making plans to enjoy what time I had left. Looking back, I can't help but crack up. We both do. We went from zero to a hundred in a matter of seconds.

Should you share? I think everyone needs to walk that out personally. You know who will react with faith and who will react with doubt, and you don't need the latter. You know who you can trust. You know who you want to pray for you. You know who you want in your journey. And yes, it is a journey. Who do you want to grip tightly and have as your soldier-in-arms? I did share the news with a few, but I was selective. I knew I needed to stay focused. I knew I needed to stay strong. Frantic people can't add to that equation; they only subtract. But several people did find out who kept subtracting even though they thought they were adding. Thankfully, it wasn't until the end of the journey that people began to talk about everything that was going on in my life. That brought on a new warfare for me. People invading my privacy. People wanting to know everything. People wanting me to talk and share. People wanting to offer advice that I didn't need or saying things that I didn't want to hear.

> I knew I needed to stay strong. Frantic people can't add to that equation; they only subtract.

Now let me shift gears and offer some godly wisdom to you if you ever find out about a friend going through a similar struggle. Let me share a few things you should *never* say to those who are facing a devastating sickness. For instance, the phrase, "Have you tried . . . ?" (Fill in the blank with lots of both home-grown and traditional cures.) First of all, chances are the answer is probably, "Yes." Most people who are suffering with sickness have tried pretty much everything imaginable to get better. Yes, I drank carrot, beet, and ginger juice. It was horrible to me. Did I stop sugar? Yes, I know that sugar feeds cancer. Yes, I lathered strange herbs in a paste on myself. Did I take Epsom salt baths to remove toxins? Yes! And I looked like a raisin from head to toe. I read the pamphlets handed to me by well-meaning strangers. But I did not eat the strange fruit that some lady told me was hundreds of years old and a medical cure-all. First, have you eaten this? And second, are you a doctor? Chances are, the answer to both questions would have been, "No."

Let's cover another one that tops the list, "Everything happens for a reason." As intelligent people, we want to be able to make sense out of everything. People would often try and remind me that my suffering might have a greater purpose or that it is occurring to teach me a lesson that will make me a better person. Well, honestly, I thought I was a good person. However, in the midst of all my doubts and fears, I didn't want or need to be reminded that I might not be or that I needed more work. It can also be misinterpreted to mean that I was *meant* to get sick, or even that I deserved it. So, if you don't mind, think twice before you share your well-intentioned wisdom! All of this might be true. But at that moment, I was not thinking about some mysterious *reason for it all*. I was merely trying to survive.

Never, ever say, "My friend or family member had cancer, and this is what he or she did." You are only trying to help, I understand, but keep in mind that many illnesses don't have a one-size-fits-all cure. While your mother's, friend's, cousin's husband could have been diagnosed with the same ailment as the person you are speaking with, it's very possible their symptoms weren't exactly the same, and he or she may have been on a completely different path. Cancer is an individual struggle. Although advice can be good (sometimes), you must be very sensitive to the person's wants and needs. It is usually a good policy to ask permission *before* you start sharing your suggestions. That way, you throw the ball in their court. That's respectful and kind.

One of the worst things that I heard more than once during my journey was someone relating how a friend or relative had the same diagnosis, but (without a blink of the eye would add) he or she died. What? Did you just actually say that to me? At that moment, I could hear my own funeral music playing. I could smell the roses on my casket. And worst of all, I could see Mike and my children without me. Any faith that I had mustered was reduced to dust. These words should never—absolutely never—be spoken to someone in the midst of the battle of his or her life.

Once a person recovers, don't ever inform that man or woman that you knew someone who had the same ailment, and it came back a second time "with a vengeance." Why would you be that insensitive?

Now let me share some things you should say to, or do for, someone struggling with a life-threatening disease.

Find a concrete way to support your friends or loved ones facing this kind of dilemma and do it. Some people may not feel comfortable asking for help, or the list of things they need help with may seem too long and overwhelming. But just forge ahead and be there for them. Some of the simplest things can make the biggest impact.

Here's a short list of suggestions:

Volunteer to drive—Ask them if you can drive them to their appointments. When treatment is over, drive them to checkups and scans. They may not show it, but cancer patients often have a lot of anxiety about these appointments, even years after treatment. I do, every time I go to the oncology center. A friendly face and someone to talk to can make a big difference.

Have a plan for refreshments—Mike and I had a ritual after treatments, food and drink. Sometimes, it was just Starbucks because I couldn't stand the smell of food. But it was comforting to know, as soon as the session was over, there was a plan.

Be a good sounding board—Just sit with your friend who is struggling and listen. Don't offer advice or recommendations unless asked. Instead, listen to their concerns, acknowledge that cancer sucks, and offer a shoulder to cry on. And if the person doesn't feel like talking, sit there with them quietly. There is a lot of power in simply being present. Many times after my treatments, I would lay on the office couch and Vicki would sit with me. If we talked, it was okay. If we didn't, it was okay. Just her presence made me happy and made me feel less alone.

Stay connected—Send encouraging texts, emails, cards, and from time to time, make phone calls, etc. Let them know you're thinking of them. My friend, Sandra, sent me cards. It was the most amazing thing. On the worst of days, a beautiful envelope would be in the mail. And there it was, a card from Sandra. The words would encourage me, give me strength, and most of all, make me feel loved. You don't have to invade someone's privacy to be a blessing. A card in the mail, a text with a funny meme, or a simple email can make a bad day better. I told you I had problems with sharing my life. But acts of kindness like these helped to restore me.

Don't treat them differently—Remember that most cancer patients don't want to be treated differently just because they have cancer. Talk to your friend or loved one like you did before. Tell jokes, talk about what's going on in the neighborhood, in the church, at your kids' school, on your favorite TV shows, movies, etc. It can help take their minds off the disease. Cancer was devouring so much of my life. It was wonderful to talk about other things. It was wonderful to act normal. It wasn't fake or living in denial. It was simply a celebration of life.

Most of all, sincerely pray—Pray like you never have before. I needed it. I was swimming in an ocean of doubt and fear. The prayers of the saints were a life preserver for me more than once. On every social media post when someone discloses a medical condition, people immediately comment, "I'll pray for you." Some people practice what they preach and actually kneel down and say a prayer, but many just use that phrase. It is just the first thing that comes to mind. While the intention may be there, it can come off as insincere. Sometimes, when people would say, "I'm praying for you," I would say, "Please, please, do." Prayer can change things. I know when my mom or Mike would lay their hands on me and pray, I could feel the power of intercession. Many times, I would lay down by my mom and say, "Do you think I'll live?" Of course," she would say, "I prayed!" And then, I would believe again.

The worst thing you can possibly do if a person you care about is sick is nothing at all. Ghosting the person or not checking in on them can make them feel incredibly isolated. I had people that I shared with, people that I trusted, people that I thought loved me, who from the moment I told them simply 'checked out.' No calls, no texts, no emails, no cards. Their silence broke my heart. Later, they told me they couldn't face it, so they ignored me. Thank you for that! I was facing death, and you couldn't face me? So please no ghosting, no ignoring, and no checking out.

> The worst thing you can possibly do if a person you care about is sick is nothing at all.

There are tears in sharing, especially when you share with the wrong ones. Later, when the subject of my season of sickness came up, some people said they didn't know what to say. Cowardly! They just didn't want to face it. Selfish! They were afraid they would say the wrong thing. Perfect love casts out fear! I needed their love and support, and your friends and loved ones need you.

Check in with the sick to let them know you are thinking about them and wanting to know how they are doing. When you avoid talking about the illness, it gives the other person the impression he or she may be burdening you by talking about their illness, leaving that struggling person feeling even more abandoned or alienated. We should never do anything to make people feel this way. We are called to be encouragers!

Now, I share my whole story. I feel like my journey has enabled me to help others. I have learned valuable lessons during my tears of sharing. Tears that washed away my distrust. Tears that cleansed my heart. Sharing is what I do now. Time and time again, I share. I do it to encourage, to give strength to others, and to show that they can win—even in the biggest battles of life.

Sharing Scriptures

1 Thessalonians 5:11

Therefore comfort each other and edify one another, just as you also are doing.

Romans 12:15

Rejoice with those who rejoice, and weep with those who weep.

Galatians 6:2

Bear one another's burdens, and so fulfill the law of Christ.

Matthew 18:20 (KJV)

"For where two or three are gathered together in my name, there am I in the midst of them."

Sharing Quotes

"We are not cisterns made for hoarding, we are channels made for sharing." —Billy Graham

"Love only grows by sharing. You can only have more for yourself by giving it away to others." —Brian Tracy

"I believe that when things are a mess, we need others to know what we are thinking, feeling, or doing. We must share our feelings with people who will not reprimand us for our thoughts. We need to share these feelings with someone who will encourage us to move forward." —David DeNotaris

"There is no greater agony than bearing an untold story inside you." —Maya Angelou

"*Tell the story of the mountain you climbed. Your words could become a page in someone else's survival guide.*"
—Morgan Harper Nichols

"*You have two hands. One is to help yourself, the second, to help others.*"—Anonymous

"*Have you ever read or heard someone's story and said, 'That's exactly what I needed to hear today'? Your story will do that for someone else.*"—Anonymous

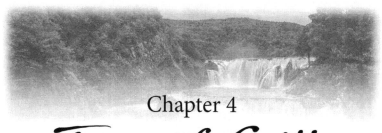

Chapter 4

Tears of Faith

The Bible says that faith is the substance of the things you hope for. It is the evidence of things not seen. In other words, faith brings those things into your life that you desire. The very fact that it resides in your heart is the evidence that the object of your faith is coming your direction. Notice this verse starts by saying, "Now faith." It's not "later" faith or "one day" faith. It is faith for today, faith for right now. So, what does it mean to have "now" faith? The basic definition of faith, according to the Bible, is simply believing in God's goodness and believing that He rewards the people who seek after Him. It's taking His Word as truth—right now. I thought I walked in that kind of faith. I believed that God was working all things out for my good. And I was seeking Him. Then, a doctor would almost destroy my faith instantly with his words. How could that happen?

When struggling with cancer, there are times you can feel very confident that you have 'that kind' of faith; you can see God working in your life. But then the doctor shows you a scan, or the side effects come, or your loved ones become distant, or the tests results are not what you expected. At times such as these, it's easy to wonder, "Do I really have faith? Where did I miss it?"

I might not have always felt it. But deep inside, I always knew it. God was still for me. Tears were running down my cheeks. My faith was shaken, but it was still there. There is no radiation room, doctor's office, chemo chair, or lonely night where your faith is not available. It can be a "now" faith. Do not let the pain and fear that breed in these kinds of places replace your knowledge that God is in charge. I know this is hard. I am a living testament to this. No matter what has happened to you in the past or what is going on in your life right now, it has no power to keep you from having an amazing future if you will walk by faith in God. God loves you! He wants you to live with victory over disease so you can possess His promises for your life today! Dare to rise up by faith and say, "I shall not die, but live" (Psalms 118:17).

I know that cancer or any sickness can too easily throw a life out of control. Before the fateful day, I had plans. I had plans for our ministry, my marriage, my children, and suddenly, there was a shift in all those plans to include the requirements of this assault on my body. Cancer is very demanding of your time, your energy, your focus, and your emotions. When people say, "Everything changed when I heard it was cancer," they're not just talking about the changes in their body. They're talking about the changes in their lives. They are talking about the changes in everything. Cancer brings us face-to-face with the lack of control we have in our day-to-day existence. But it also brings us to the fact of who is really in control. God is. I thought I was in control. I was doing all the right things. I was working in the ministry. I was raising good kids. I was a great wife. Doesn't that sound like someone in control? But when it was all said and done, at that moment in my life, two things were controlling my every move, cancer and God. Thankfully, God was bigger. If there was a passage of Scripture I clung to tenaciously, it was Psalm 27:13 (KJV):

I had fainted, unless I had believed to see the goodness of the LORD in the land of the living.

Even though I expected to see His goodness poured out, I was still struggling. My faith was on again and off again. Things were spinning out of control. Doctor visits were every day. More tests, more blood work, and more sitting in waiting rooms with all the sick people. But wait, I *was* one of those sick people. It was a hard concept to grasp. They were me and I was them. You could see it on their faces. They were thinking the same thoughts as me. Life . . . Death . . . Past . . . Present . . . and . . . is there even a Future?

It was Thanksgiving week. The kids were excited. Black Friday was coming up. I always made a big party out of that special time. We always went with a group. Fight the Black Friday crowd for nothing. Laugh, sing, and dance through the stores. I didn't want the kids to miss it. But the doctors were very stern about a PET scan needing to be done immediately. I hate to say it, but I think I was still in a bit of denial. I went to the doctor on Wednesday of that week, hopeful that just maybe they would say it was all a big mistake. My hope was crushed. I began to cry.

There was the most wonderful girl there. Her name was Tori. She was in scheduling. She cried with me. I don't know why. We just sat there, tears streaming down our faces. She told me things were not always as bad as they seemed. You just have to have faith. She told me the doctor wanted the scan immediately, but everything was shutting down for the holidays. I was already so low in my spirit. But with her persistent way, she booked me on Black Friday. How, I don't even know. Looking back now, I just laugh. "Black Friday Special - one pet scan coming right up."

We hit the stores with all the kids in tow. Mike drove. How much does he love me? This was his first ever Black Friday. He would rather fight the devil than shop. But he knew I couldn't possibly pull this off alone. I cried as we pulled up to each stop. Would this be my last Black Friday? Who would take the kids next year? It was really remarkable, only Mike and I realized how hard this shopping trip was. I deserved an Oscar for my acting in the movie *"Cancer Can't Cancel Black Friday."*

Zion Seth and all his friends shopped for hours. Destiny and I enjoyed drinking coffee and eating. Mike sat in the van and worked. It was the perfect trip, or so everyone thought. I hid my tears that day from everyone. I pretended that everything was wonderful. But inside I was so shaken.

We dropped the kids off at home early on Friday morning with their sweet grandmother who lived with us. All night shopping, they were ready to crash. Mike and I left immediately for the hospital. It was cold and damp outside. But inside the hospital, it was colder and more damp. A skeleton crew was there. It was, after all, the holidays. We waited for the unknown. We waited for my name to be called. The imaging department was closed for Thanksgiving. It was just me and one elderly gentleman present. I wondered if we were in the same boat. The moments of waiting are excruciating. All you can think about is whether or not you will have to go through chemo and radiation therapies. The waiting in the cancer journey is almost like walking across hot coals while wearing shoes soaked with gasoline (well, not quite that bad). Nothing helps. You are constantly waiting. Waiting for appointments, waiting for scans, waiting for bloodwork, waiting for therapies . . . the list goes on and on. Waiting.

Where was my faith? Where was Mike's faith? Where was the church's faith? I felt faithless. I felt abandoned. And I believe that elderly gentlemen did, too. I could see it in his eyes. I wondered if my eyes looked like his. "Elizabeth, Elizabeth Shreve": I would hear my name called like that many more times in the next few months. Where was God? Where was my Lord, and Savior, Jesus? I'm not being negative. I am just saying, your mind begins to run away from you. The technician was a young man named Kevin. He was indifferent to me. To him, I was just a number on a band around my wrist. I felt for him. He must have drawn the short end of the stick. He had to work on this holiday. A young lady was with him. She explained a few things. I didn't really hear her. All I did hear were key words I didn't want to hear—undress, gown,

I.V., cold, dye, and don't move. There and then, in that place and that moment, I and the elderly gentleman were side-by-side. A curtain hung between us, open just enough for us to see each other's faces. But there were no words to be spoken. Just the sad empty eyes that we looked at each other with.

My time came. While I was feeling lost and faithless, Kevin explained how this big tunnel looking machine worked. You lay here. You don't move. There will be loud clicking noises. Then we all go home. Yay! Thanks, Kevin. Laying flat on a big table is scary. Those clicking noises are terrifying. Where was faith again? Hope, now, substance, evidence? I felt like the father of the sick child in Mark 9:24 (MKJV), "Lord, I believe. Help my unbelief."

As the machine started moving, I started crying. Not loud sobbing. But gentle tears streaming down my face. "God, where are you? What did I do wrong? Why would you punish me? I promise, I'll do better. I'll do more." Wet, hot tears dripping down on the table.

Kevin spoke clearly and sharply, "You cannot move or we will have to start over. You must be perfectly still, or the imaging will not be correct." I know he didn't intend to sound so cold and mean. But he did sound that way. Looking back now, I can sympathize. I'm sure he didn't want to be working on the holidays. He wasn't a bad guy, but he probably had never been in a fight for his life either. I couldn't stop the crying. The slab was so cold. So, I laid there silently weeping and trying not to move. And I felt so alone. Maybe you have never felt like God has forgotten or forsaken you. Let me tell you from experience, it is not a nice feeling. "Where are you God? Do those promises about healing apply to me?" Sigh....

But then, what a surprise! I heard music! Orchestra music! And a choir! Thankful, for the distraction from my rant with God. I thought, *I know that song*. The words started ringing in my mind:

I will cherish the old rugged cross.
Till my trophies at last I lay down.
I will cling to the old rugged cross
And exchange it someday for a crown.

I couldn't help it. I moved. Much to Kevin's disliking, I lifted my hand to praise God. He immediately reprimanded me. "Don't move! Be perfectly still!" But I couldn't help myself. Kevin, I know that song. I was singing it. I was filled with the song in my broken spirit. Needless to say, he was not happy with me. He pulled me out of the machine. With such a disappointed look, he explained to me again, "Please do not move. Please be perfectly still. It messes up the image if you move." But I wanted him to know. I knew that song. It was a song from my childhood. We sang it all the time. It is about the love of Christ and His sacrifice on the cross. Kevin was not impressed.

Then, to my shock he said, "Ma'am, there is no music in this area. Now, please be still." I wanted to say, "But I'm hearing music," however, I held my words back (a real feat for me). Then my faith soared when I thought, *I'm hearing music where none is being played. What a miracle!* But then I lapsed into unbelief, thinking, *Great, the cancer has traveled to my brain. I have both breast and brain cancer now.*

> Then my faith soared when I thought, *I'm hearing music where none is being played. What a miracle!*

So, Kevin put me in the scanner a second time. I waited in anticipation for *The Old Rugged Cross*. Nothing! Yep! It's gone to my brain! I'm hearing things now. You might as well put me down. Then, the music started again, but not the first song. It was a more modern song:

Here I am to worship; here I am to bow down,
Here I am to say that You're my God
You're altogether lovely, altogether worthy,
Altogether wonderful to me.

I'll never know how much it cost,
To see my sin upon that cross.
I'll never know how much it cost,
To see my sin upon that cross.

Here I am to worship; here I am to bow down,
Here I am to say that You're my God.
You're altogether lovely, altogether worthy,
Altogether wonderful to me.[1]

That was it. A second witness (God usually moves that way).

Full-on worship started in me. As I listened to the orchestra and choir rendition, I was singing out loud with all my heart. My tears of doubt had transformed into tears of faith. I knew that God was speaking to me. I was not abandoned. I was not alone in this battle. He was letting me know in a unique way, in language I could understand, that through this I was going to learn that He died for my victory, that I could cling to the cross and win this battle. Not only that—through all of this, I was going to learn to worship in the midst of the storm and be an example to others of how to respond to struggles with a heart that praises God anyway.

The Old Rugged Cross and *Here I Am to Worship* were going to be my battle hymns. They would remind me every day, from that point forward, that I would cherish Him more, and not draw back—I would love Him more and not doubt. Instead, I determined to worship Him more, praising Him in advance for my miracle.

As you might expect, the young technician was furious. He pulled me out of the machine so fast. Looking at me with piercing eyes, he tensely informed, "Mrs. Shreve. I want to go home. I want to enjoy my holiday. Can you please stop!" I couldn't help it. Faith showed up and I was ready to proclaim it. My long-lost friend, faith, had decided to take me by the hand, and I was in much need of its companionship.

"Buddy, did you hear the music that time?"

"No music, ma'am. We have no music in the scan area. Do I need to call your doctor? Do you have a therapist? Maybe today is too stressful for you to get a scan."

Then, unexpectedly, I felt the Spirit of God move on me to pry into his personal life spiritually—so I asked, "Son, do you know the Lord?"

He was so taken aback by my question, but I had to share the rescue of my faith with him. I had just experienced a visitation from the Most High inside that big machine. I heard music that came to me supernaturally, as if it was from another world. Faith really is the substance of things hoped for and the evidence of things not seen. It worked amazingly. Hope and evidence came and had a party with me inside the scan. And we were ready to share the glory.

"Son, do you know the Lord?" Yep, just as I thought, he was not walking with God. But he knew Him once. My response? Let me reintroduce you to the One that hung on *The Old Rugged Cross*, the One that you are going to worship from here on out.

Those two songs (that echoed from another realm) were like eagle wings to me that day. They gave me the power to soar above my battle. It's been years now (at the time of this writing), and I am still soaring.

I also learned once again that God turns curses into blessings (see Deuteronomy 23:5). He takes bad events in our lives and fills it with His purpose. Maybe, just maybe, I needed to be there for the technician's sake, more than my own.

God is really a genius at weaving these "good" things together for those who believe.

faith Scriptures

Hebrews 11:1

Now faith is the substance of things hoped for, the evidence of things not seen.

Psalms 46:10

Be still, and know that I am God; I will be exalted among the nations, I will be exalted in the earth!

John 7:38

"He who believes in Me, as the Scripture has said, out of his heart will flow rivers of living water."

Romans 10:17

So then faith comes by hearing, and hearing by the word of God.

Mark 5:36 (NIV)

Overhearing what they said, Jesus told him, "Don't be afraid; just believe."

Romans 10:9 (NIV)

If you declare with your mouth, "Jesus is Lord," and believe in your heart that God raised him from the dead, you will be saved.

2 Corinthians 5:7

For we walk by faith, not by sight.

Hebrews 11:6 (NIV)

And without faith it is impossible to please God, because anyone who comes to him must believe that he exists and that he rewards those who earnestly seek him.

Mark 11:22-24

So Jesus answered and said to them, "Have faith in God. For assuredly, I say to you, whoever says to this mountain, 'Be removed and be cast into the sea,' and does not doubt in his heart, but believes that those things he says will be done, he will have whatever he says. Therefore I say to you, whatever things you ask when you pray, believe that you receive them, and you will have them."

1 Corinthians 2:5 (ESV)

That your faith might not rest in the wisdom of men but in the power of God.

Matthew 21:22 (ESV)

"And whatever you ask in prayer, you will receive, if you have faith."

Luke 1:37 (ESV)

"For nothing will be impossible with God."

1 Corinthians 16:13 (NIV)

Be on your guard; stand firm in the faith; be courageous; be strong.

Faith Quotes

"Faith is taking the first step even when you don't see the whole staircase." —Martin Luther King Jr.

"Only in the darkness can you see the stars." —Martin Luther King Jr.

My faith didn't remove the pain, but it got me through the pain. Trusting God didn't diminish or vanquish the anguish, but it enabled me to endure it." —Robert Rogers

"*True peace comes from knowing that God is in control.*" —Anonymous

"*If you lose faith, you lose all.*" —Eleanor Roosevelt

"*Faith is unseen but felt, faith is strength when we feel we have none, faith is hope when all seems lost.*"
—Catherine Pulsifer

"*Faith and prayer are the vitamins of the soul; man cannot live in health without them.*" —Mahalia Jackson

Chapter 5

Tears of Disappointment

So, I had a supernatural revelation on Black Friday. I was expecting a total miracle. Healed, that was me. God visited me in the machine. He played me two prophetic songs. I witnessed to a young man. Life was right back on track. So ready, set, and go. No cancer. I would tell others of this miraculous healing on Thanksgiving. I will learn from this scare and take better care of myself. Definitely, I was healed. It was a test of faith. And I passed with flying colors. Yay, me and Yay, God!

On Monday, I called the doctors excited. After all, I had my miracle! He didn't sound as enthusiastic. He didn't say anything like what I anticipated. Cancer was still his main subject. The scans aren't back. We should go ahead and schedule surgery. The scans will help us to determine the margins. Pathology will be in the room with us.

Wait, miracle visitation! Surely, the doctor could sense my healing. Songs in a scan machine. Young man getting saved. Can't he recognize my miracle. But the more information that was flooding me, the more disappointed I became. The definition of disappointment is unhappiness from the failure of something hoped for or expected to happen. I anticipated the staff saying, "Have a happy life. You're a walking miracle. Everything is clear." But all I was hearing was: surgery, radiation, pathology, scan, reconstruction, follow-up, medication. There was that wet liquid pouring out of my eyes again. I thought I was healed. I thought this journey was over. I thought . . .

Whoever said, "There's no way to make time stand still" clearly never had to endure the excruciating wait for scan results. You'd think it would come instantaneously. The doctor said it could be days. They would have a team of doctors reviewing my case. All the "ologists" would be there. In an age of instant everything, cancer patients being told that the scans from the cutting-edge technology that is creating real-time images of our insides will be available in anything less than a second defies logic and seems unnecessarily cruel. But everything about cancer is cruel. Doctors are not, but the disease holds hostages. When you have a plan in your mind for your "best life" or what the future holds, but it doesn't match your present circumstances, that creates a lot of confusion. You can quickly go from plan to pain.

I underwent a PET scan on Black Friday. And I assure you that not only did time stand still, but it seemed to even move backward. During those frozen moments in time, it's hard to think about plans for a future that may not be. I was ready to tell the world of my miracle. My world was ready to tell me about my treatments.

> Faith means living with uncertainty—feeling your way through life, letting your heart guide you like a lantern in the dark.

When the word finally came that the scan showed a mass, the movie of my life kicked into a freeze frame. It's similar to those tense moments when the internet starts buffering. You just sit there waiting. Sitting back down to lunch with my Mike, we ate in silence as if it were our last, and first, meal. It was the last supper and Judas (cancer) was dipping his bread in the cup.

There was a strange silence between us as if the celebration of the miracle had been rained on by the unnecessary struggle and uncertainty of what might come next. Faith means living with uncertainty—feeling your way through life, letting your heart guide you like a lantern in the dark. But when disappointment is raging, it is hard to hold on to faith.

Mike had to go back on the road and preach. He didn't want to. He would never leave my side. But how would we survive financially. How would my children live? Plus, I am a believer in holding to your responsibilities. Also, I believed that if Mike was faithful to God, that God would be faithful to us. I told him not to worry. After all, I am a strong and independent woman. I could still handle everything all by myself. This is one of the lies that cancer fighters will tell themselves. Because you *cannot* face this alone. But I was determined to keep doing everything myself. I would get the kids to school, work at the ministry, buy the groceries, fix the meals, and everything that I needed to do.

I was in total denial. I was so disappointed that I was not healed. I thought the mass would be gone. But it wasn't. It was there, laughing at me. The more my mind dwelt on it, the more powerful it became. I started feeling it whenever I moved. I didn't want to shower because it was there. I didn't want to change clothes, because it was there—staring me in the face. I was discouraged and alone. Did I let Mike know how I was feeling? No. Because he had a life and a calling. I didn't want to be a burden. I didn't want to drag him down with me.

My pit was getting deeper and deeper. But I didn't want anyone to drown with me. So, I laughed. I smiled. I joked. I cooked. I went to ballet practice with Destiny. I was at Tae Kwon Do with Zion Seth. People would say, "How are you?" "Fine," would be my declaration. Because I was acting fine, everyone thought I was. But disappointment and discouragement are silent killers. They sneak up on you. They stalk you. Friends and family can't recognize a disappointed, discouraged actor.

We perform our part well. We can stand on the stage and thank everyone for the trophy. But the truth is strangling us.

Alone and discouraged, I took the kids to school and headed for an appointment at the clinic. I remember crying all the way down to Chattanooga. Tears of disappointment were drowning my heart. My mind just kept saying, "You are alone! You have always been alone. Growing up, you were alone. You are alone in the church. You were meant to be alone. You have no one. You never have. Where is God? Where is Mike?"

Disappointment and discouragement have a companion called loneliness. They are all best friends. Everyone who is facing a life-threatening disease feels the pain of being alone. Go sit in one of the waiting rooms; look at the faces of people. You can see it. You may not feel it, but you can see it. Though you are not physically alone, mentally there is no one in sight.

> Disappointment and discouragement have a companion called loneliness.

The doctor's appointment went as usual. Scheduling, poking, looking, no clothes, ugly gown, more people looking. Now, they have to touch. Why? Does everyone have to handle my naked body with their hands? Take pictures! Surgery needs to be scheduled. Do I schedule it according to Mike's preaching schedule? We never know how much pressure we can handle until it comes. "Please sign here. Where is your husband? Is someone with you?" "No, I am all alone. All alone," it was like an echo in a giant cavern. "Alone . . . Alone . . . Alone. You're always alone."

I gathered my things, trying not to burst into tears. At least, in the clinic you don't have to pretend to be happy. You can just walk like a zombie. You can nod your head and not speak. Most of the people there are in the fight for their lives. So, it is okay to look like you just got hit by a train. Because everyone else either has been or is going to be in train wreck situations just as devastating. The waiting room of a cancer clinic can be one of the loneliest places in the world.

The booming voice of my mind was saying, "Alone, alone, alone." Then the craziest song popped into my head, "All by Myself" by Eric Carmen. Do you remember it? In the lyrics, he talked about how lonely, distant, obscure, and insecure he felt—because he was all by himself.

The mind is a crazy thing. I probably hadn't heard that song in years. But right when I didn't need it, there it was. Booming in my ears. Discouraging me even more. God had sent two songs to encourage me; then the enemy sent one song to discourage me.

Walking to the elevator, I was thinking, *I am all alone. I am probably going to die alone.* The bell sounded. The doors to the elevator opened. I stepped in and pushed the button. Dazed and confused. Discouraged and calloused. When I heard a small sound, I looked over in the elevator. A woman was there. My first thought was, *She better not speak to me. I am in no mood to talk about the weather or any other mundane thing.* She was unusual looking. She was small in stature. She wore a red button-up skirt. Her shirt was like from the early 60s. It was long sleeve and high neck. It had ruffles around the sleeves and neck. A little red shoestring was tied around her neck in a perfect little bow. Her hair was in a high Pentecostal-looking bun. Silver was her hair color. Little red flat shoes finished off her fashion statement. She was pristine. She was elegant looking in an old-fashioned way. I grew up with this kind of woman.

But then she spoke. Her voice was sweet but powerful. It was the voice of many waters coming out of her little, perfect lips. She took a step toward me. I stepped back. The elevator was suspended in time. It was just two floors to go down, but it felt like slow motion had kicked in. She stepped closer and said, "You look like you need a hug." Well, first, I am not a hugger. I don't like my personal space compromised. I don't like to be touched. But she hugged me so quickly, I couldn't get away. Her hug was soothing, calming, and strangely—electrifying. It was as if that hug was reaching into the dark pit of discouragement that I had fallen into. She held me tight. My defenses broke down. I melted in her arms. Her kindness was healing my lost soul. She felt like home. Or at least what I thought home should feel like. She smelled like the most beautiful fragrance. I had never smelled it before. I was used to the scent of rubbing alcohol and sterile swabs. She was breathtaking. But it didn't stop there. She was shorter than me, so she stood on her toes to reach up to my ear. She whispered in the kindest way, "You are not alone. And everything will turn out alright."

Unbelievable! She had just erased all my fears, doubts, and discouragement. My tears were full of peace and faith. I couldn't believe what she said. The elevator doors opened. I was shaken. I stepped out and the doors closed. I wanted to say, "Thank you." I was awestruck. I looked around and she was not there. I wanted her to hug me again. I wanted her number. I wanted what she had. I not only wanted it, I needed it. I needed that kind of peace. I wanted her to whisper in my ear something else encouraging.

> She whispered in the kindest way, "You are not alone. And everything will turn out alright."

I jumped on the elevator again. She must be a volunteer. The second floor staff told me that no one like that was there. Elevator again. The third floor staff said they had never seen an older woman like that. Ever. I went to valet parking; surely, they would have seen her. No lady in a red skirt.

"Puzzled" is not a strong enough word for what I was feeling. I called Mike. He could hear the excitement in my voice. This lady in red, she hugged me and whispered in my ear words that were exactly fitted to what I had been thinking. She destroyed my discouragement with a whisper. I was talking so fast. Mike could barely get a word in. "Honey, do you think she was an angel?" he asked. Angels don't visit people like me. "Honey, do you think you had an angelic visitation?" Angels have better things to do than whisper in my ear. But then, I felt it. I knew it.

God had given me another visitation, a supernatural confirmation. The Lord in all his kindness sent a little lady dressed in red with a high, beehive hairdo to encourage me. She knew if she whispered, I would hear. She knew I was lonely. She hugged my loneliness away. Her voice penetrated the dark place in my life. She brought me to the light. I will forever be grateful for that elevator ride. I look for her every time I step on that same elevator. I miss her. I miss the peace I felt. Thank you, God, for sending her to me. It changed my course. It set me on a different path. It helped me survive.

Overcoming Disappointment Scriptures

Joshua 1:9

> "Have I not commanded you? Be strong and of good courage; do not be afraid, nor be dismayed, for the Lord your God is with you wherever you go."

Isaiah 40:31

> But those who wait on the Lord shall renew their strength; they shall mount up with wings like eagles, they shall run and not be weary, they shall walk and not faint.

Isaiah 43:2

> "When you pass through the waters, I will be with you; and through the rivers, they shall not overflow you. When you walk through the fire, you shall not be burned, nor shall the flame scorch you."

Psalms 55:22

> Cast your burden on the Lord, and He shall sustain you; He shall never permit the righteous to be moved.

Psalms 120:1 (ESV)

> In my distress I called to the LORD, and he answered me.

Philippians 4:19

> And my God shall supply all your need according to His riches in glory by Christ Jesus.

Luke 12:6–7 (NIV)

> "Are not five sparrows sold for two pennies? Yet not one of them is forgotten by God. Indeed, the very hairs of your head are all numbered. Don't be afraid; you are worth more than many sparrows."

Mark 10:27 (ESV)

> *Jesus looked at them and said, "With man it is impossible, but not with God. For all things are possible with God."*

Overcoming Disappointment Quotes

"Stop wishing your life was different and live the one you have, because it's the only one you have got."
—Anonymous

"Life is like riding a bicycle. To keep your balance, you must keep moving." —Albert Einstein

"Ships don't sink because of the water around them; ships sink because of the water that gets in them. Don't let what's happening around you get inside you and weigh you down." —Anonymous

"The remedy for discouragement is the Word of God. When you feed your heart and mind with its truth, you regain your perspective and find renewed strength."
—Warren Wiersbe

Chapter 6
Tears of Joy

After all the supernatural visitations, a sense of relief and joy finally came to me. I was soaring with the eagles. I sang the songs that I had heard. I looked for my angel in red. I told a few more people about what had transpired. Up until that point, I had hidden my sickness. I was ashamed that sickness had attacked me. I felt people would pity me or say that I deserved to be sick. I felt like a failure. I didn't want others to see my shame. After all, I couldn't figure out why this had happened to me. So why would they be able to discern such a thing? However, I was sensing a surge of positivity. Maybe, I would survive.

So finally, I felt encouraged.

I had not felt that emotion for a while, encouragement. It is hard to feel that when you are facing a cancer diagnosis. Everywhere I looked, I saw sick people. It's like the little boy in the movie, "The Sixth Sense." He says over and over, "I see dead people." Looking around at that time, all I saw were sick people. But my life was looking up. The light was peeking through all my dark. Light was winning!

Nothing was going to bring me down. Nothing, I say! I began to think about the future. I began to think about life, not death. I began planning a vacation, not my funeral (although, my funeral was going to be pretty awesome, if I say so myself). It is amazing how peace can come so suddenly. I thought the world was ending for me and then, all of a sudden, it was like a new beginning. Peace was sitting on the throne of my heart. Fear and doubt were in the dungeon.

Relief is defined as a feeling of reassurance and relaxation following release from anxiety or distress. Our world had been full of anxiety and distress for a while. I was constantly crying and hiding. But because of those wonderful God-moments, I was set free from the darkness. A new path was arising. The path to victory. The path to hope.

The world was blooming with roses again. I had not been able to breathe for a long time. But suddenly, I felt like a new person. Light had taken over the darkness. It has been said that we cannot know the light without experiencing the darkness. But it's also true that encounters with darkness and with light can both be great teachers. The lessons I was learning, and was going to learn, would change me forever. But when you are going through this storm, you aren't really thinking of lessons and teachers. Matter of fact, you couldn't care less. Keep your lessons and your teachers. You are thinking of surviving. You are thinking of what you will face the next day. You are thinking of how to hold on.

You are really not prepared for all the steps in this journey. Everything is left uncertain. Thankfully, I was walking in relief and peace. My faith was on a high. Stepping into the future with God on my side and the lady in red, success was imminent.

God was ordering my steps every day. Favor was my side-kick. It seemed like everyone that I came in contact with was an encourager. I was singing that old song—"I'm Walking on Sunshine," especially the line that says, *"Don't it feel good?"*

And it did feel good. I was believing for the best. But you must realize that even when you are feeling good, there will be moments when you lapse into anxiety. I tried to keep those damaging feelings at bay. People can be helpful, but sometimes they can be a hindrance. You have to watch who speaks into your life during crisis times like this. You can't allow the negative influences in. That was one of my biggest errors during that season in my life. People can rob you of your joy and peace. All it takes is one negative thought, and you can lose the ground that you have taken. So, as I was still singing my sunshine song, there were people and things that showed up like dark storm clouds. My focus should have stayed on the

> People can rob you of your joy and peace. All it takes is one negative thought, and you can lose the ground that you have taken.

Lord. But little by little, my song began to fade.

There was still a shadow hanging over me. I could feel it. I dreaded answering my phone: another doctor, another appointment, another test . . . the "another" list kept growing. There was a war going on inside me. My mind, heart, and body were fighting. Darkness was trying to creep back in. Scriptures were put up everywhere in our house. We saturated everything with the Word of God. Worship music was put on a loop. Darkness couldn't get back in; we wouldn't let it. But remember that war I was talking about. It was raging. Fear over faith, darkness over light, evil over good, and sickness over health. The more I tried to be positive, the harder it was to maintain that mindset. Crying out to the Lord one night, I begged to live. I pleaded with God to let me see my children get married and have babies. I wanted to grow old with the love of my life, Mike. The voices of hope were disappearing. My lady in red was not showing herself. At times, I even wondered if that really happened. My sense of relief was fading. I didn't want it to disappear. I waged war on my enemies.

You know how this book was birthed? At a certain point, I felt my spirit getting really low. Joy and relief were backing off, retreating from my 'war-zone.' I knew I needed some strong Christian resources: books, videos and CDs, anything that would keep my faith strong. I needed the testimonies of others who had walked this road. I wanted the stories of victory, the witness of those who had conquered. I desired encouraging words from women of God who would cause me to rise up as a warrior. So, off to the bookstore I went.

The greeter met me with such a sweet smile and the welcoming statement, "Can I help you?" I mustered up the courage to say those horrible words, "I have cancer. Do you have any books that would help me?" A look of fright came over her face. I could see it. Just so everyone knows, cancer is not contagious. So please don't look at us differently as if we are. You can't catch it by shaking our hand.

She led me to a bottom shelf, hidden under all the fitness, self-help, religious dieting, and health books. It was like the books were ashamed to be seen. Unfortunately, I could relate. I wanted to hide, too. I was ashamed to be seen. I was ashamed to tell others my plight. These were probably the books for me, since they were hiding, too. After all, who would write such a thing. Who would admit that they were diagnosed? But I knew that I needed to be encouraged. I needed books full of scriptures and stories of deliverance. I quickly gathered up five or six, paid for them and left. I can remember holding them to my chest. Afraid of what they would say and yet hoping and praying for words that could soothe my soul.

I just knew those books would provide much-needed relief. They would speak positive thoughts and give insightful clues on how to navigate this journey. My heart would feel the warmth of their words. My mind would find peace in their versions of the journey. I was so ready to have my faith lifted, I drove home quickly. I felt excitement, a sense of anticipation. With the fireplace roaring, laying on the floor, I began my adventure into the world of cancer books. Nope, that one was not uplifting. Wow, that one was like the Titanic. Surely, the next one. "Help me, Lord," that one was based on the story of Job. Where is the healing? Where are the ladies in red? Where are the songs from the pet scan? This is not what I was expecting. They spoke of hair falling out, vomiting non-stop, mastectomy, double mastectomy, and walking up to the door of death—all the things I didn't want to read about.

Mike came in from work to find me curled up on the floor crying. Luckily, my children were not at home to see this complete meltdown. How did I go from relief to despair? What happened? It was not my anticipated emotion. These books were supposed to be my shield and buckler. Instead, they were a sword that pierced my soul. Yes, the authors survived. But I wanted to hear that survival wasn't that hard. I wanted to hear it was a walk in the park. Could we please sugarcoat it?

Those books were returned quickly. Mike refused to keep them in the house. Right then I heard the words in my heart, "You will write a book. It will tell the truth, but it will also give relief to those who need it." No, cancer isn't a walk in the park. But you can watch the kites fly in the wind, the dogs catch a frisbee, and see families enjoying life in the outdoors. Life is all about perspective. It is how you look at things, the slant with which you interpret things, the lens through which you see things. A sense of relief brings joy and happiness, but how can you hold on to it?

> Right then I heard the words in my heart, "You will write a book. It will tell the truth, but it will also give relief to those who need it."

First, we have to break down the difference between happiness and joy. Happiness is linked to external circumstances and joy is a more internal, deeply-rooted thing that is less easily shaken. Listen, I want both. I want to be happy and I want to be joyful. During that season, I wanted to feel both happiness and joy. I wanted relief that stayed.

We must speak words of encouragement to ourselves, just like we would water a little plant. Then happiness takes root, grows shoots, and becomes a tree that crowds out the weeds of doubt and fear. It can even uproot despair. What we water grows stronger. What we water is what will grow. Water the fear, and the fear grows like a plant in a sun-drenched but moisture-filled greenhouse. Water the truth, and you'll find yourself in an increasing state of hope, joy, and peace. It's a choice. I know it doesn't always feel like a choice, and it is a practice that you will hone over time with patience and commitment, but in the end, it is a choice. You choose to allow fear to run the show or to take the risk and open your heart to joy.

Joy is something so hard to explain to this world because it is dependent on God. It does not come from the soul, where happiness camps (the human part of us); it comes from the spirit (the regenerated spirit of a born-again believer) where the river of God's Spirit flows. We don't manufacture joy like we do happiness. It goes deeper than emotion. Joy is contentment, in spite of circumstances.

But it's also true that even when we choose to be happy, or we pick up joy and wear it like a garment—life will not magically become easy. We must not fall back into old patterns. You have to stay on guard. And you will need to wrestle, question, and fight your way back again. All the way back to happy. That's okay. At least you're fighting. You're in the game, showing up. Don't wait for tomorrow. Be happy now. Find your joy now.

At the time of all this, I didn't understand that there was a difference. Relief will only come when you walk in these two truths. You will need both to endure. Happiness and joy must become best friends in your life.

Happiness depends on positive, external factors to exist. Happiness depends on what "happens" to us. We are happy when something good occurs. Even though we may seek it, desire it, pursue it, the feeling of happiness is not usually a choice we make.

Joy doesn't need a smile in order to exist, although it does feel better with one.

Joy, on the other hand, is a decision purposefully made. Joy is an attitude of the heart, present inside of us as an untapped reservoir of potential. Is it possible to feel joy in difficult times? Yes!

Joy doesn't need a smile in order to exist, although it does feel better with one. Joy can share its space with other emotions—sadness, shame or anger. Happiness can't. Happiness is not present in darkness and difficulty. Joy will never leave these low valleys (if we learn how to maintain it). Joy undergirds our spirits; it gives birth to relief, peace, and contentment. Mike has always said, "Joy is a choice." During that season in my life, I realized those words were so true.

A wise woman at the oncology department told me this, "There are three A's in cancer survival—Appetite, Activity, and Attitude." Appetite and Activity are so important. But your attitude about everything will set the course to your destination. I believe the most important is attitude. I have repeated this many, many times over the years. We cannot choose the things that happen to us. But we can choose the attitude we take toward anything that happens. Success or failure depends on your attitude. And joy is a great one to cultivate, even when it is mixed with tears.

Joy / Happiness Scriptures

Romans 15:13

Now may the God of hope fill you with all joy and peace in believing, that you may abound in hope by the power of the Holy Spirit.

1 Peter 1:8

Whom having not seen you love. Though now you do not see Him, yet believing, you rejoice with joy inexpressible and full of glory.

Psalms 16:9

Therefore my heart is glad, and my glory rejoices; my flesh also will rest in hope.

1 Thessalonians 5:16 (KJV)

Rejoice evermore.

Psalms 118:24

This is the day the LORD has made; we will rejoice and be glad in it.

Nehemiah 8:10

Then he said to them, "Go your way, eat the fat, drink the sweet, and send portions to those for whom nothing is prepared; for this day is holy to our Lord. Do not sorrow, for the joy of the LORD is your strength."

Joy / Happiness Quotes

"They say a person needs just three things to be truly happy in this world: someone to love, something to do, and something to hope for." —Tom Bodett

"I don't think of all the misery, but of the beauty that still remains." —Anne Frank, *The Diary of a Young Girl*

"One can never consent to creep when one feels an impulse to soar." —Helen Keller, *The Story of My Life*

"Joy is the infallible sign of the presence of God." —Pierre Teilhard de Chardin

"When you are joyful, when you say yes to life and have fun and project positivity all around you, you become a sun in the center of every constellation, and people want to be near you." —Shannon L. Alder

Finally I have a quote that comes from a Buddhist. Even though they do not acknowledge the God of the Bible, I felt like including this wise statement—because if a Buddhist can subscribe to this (without faith in God), how much more should we who do have faith in the God of heaven and earth.

"Walk as if you are kissing the Earth with your feet." —Thich Nhat Hanh

I'm still trying to live this way.

Chapter 7

Tears of Depression

I have always been a thrill-seeker. So, I love roller coasters. And guess what, life is like a roller coaster. You hop on thinking it is going to be so exciting. You travel up the first long rail with anticipation. You tell yourself, "This is going to be so fun." The higher you get, the more you start to reconsider your choice. Even as you climb, you begin to dread the fall. The "click, click, click" of the car on the track rings in your ears as it strains to move just a few feet higher. How far up are we? Don't ever look down! What exactly keeps this car on the rails? I am not going to lie, there is excitement: nervous energy that builds inside your heart, burning like a marshmallow on the open flame. But are you feeling the excitement, are you enjoying it? For me, I'm already two steps ahead to what I know is coming. I am preparing myself. I check to make sure the bar is intact. I look at my daughter; she is okay. I can't possibly let her know what I am thinking. I say a silent prayer, *Please God, don't let me die on this thing. I promise You; I won't subject myself to this kind of danger again.* All the time, I am trying to enjoy the ride. I want to enjoy it.

As the car tops the hill, there is a moment when we seem suspended, paused in time. I always wish, during that split second, that I could just stay there, forever if needed. It is a beautiful view. But looks can be deceiving. I know what is coming. I want to avoid what is coming. Longing for avoidance is a great trait to have at times. Unfortunately, choosing to avoid things in life is the choice to avoid living, and to avoid living is one of the saddest things of all. One of my favorite quotes is, "The saddest thing of word and pen is the phrase it might have been." You have to get on the ride to enjoy it.

> One of my favorite quotes is, "The saddest thing of word and pen is the phrase it might have been."

At the moment, at the top, I don't care that it would mean never coming down or continuing with life. I do not want to experience the drop. The drop that makes your stomach turn. The drop that makes you scream even if you try not to. The drop that causes you to either enjoy the ride or hate it. A decision must be made. And then, we are falling. I am clinging to the bar in front of me. My white knuckles are holding on for dear life. I am screaming to the top of my lungs. I'm both convinced it will never end and convinced it's going to end immediately with my sudden and excruciatingly painful death. Why did I do this? I am begging for something to stop it. I'm praying that I live through it, praying that it's over soon. And I say to myself, *I will never do this again.*

Does this sound familiar? Cancer is like a roller coaster. Any major sickness you may get is like a roller coaster. You are constantly being jerked and turned inside out. You go up, you go down. You are strapped into a car hurtling at a high rate of speed hundreds of feet in the air (or at least it feels like hundreds) with unanticipated twists and turns. You can hear the screams of those around you. The higher you rise, the further it seems you might fall. It becomes such a reliable pattern that you often learn to dread when things seem to be going really well. Instead you are always waiting—waiting for the other shoe to drop, waiting for the fall. One day, a doctor tells you it's going well. Then, the next doctor says the opposite. One day, your blood work is excellent. The next draw of blood doesn't look good at all. You are on a constant ride that never stops. The drop is always about to happen.

Roller coaster . . . Can I get off now?

I thought that with all the miraculous things that had happened to me, the ride was over. I thought that a visitation from an angel meant my healing. I believed that on my next visit to the doctor, he would gladly say with joy, "There is nothing there. Go and enjoy your life. You can tell the world about your miraculous healing." Then the doctor would get down on his knees and proclaim faith in the Lord. I would be a testament to many. I had believed this to happen several times. But instead, the call came that we were not waiting till after the holidays. The doctors had gotten together to discuss my case. Surgery needed to be done immediately. The tumor had to come out before anything else could be done. We didn't want to run the chance of it metastasizing. Waiting would not be a wise thing to do. It had to be done immediately. There was no waiting. This was serious. What?

It was like the wind had been knocked out of me. Wait, but the lady in the elevator told me everything was going to be okay. Okay? That definitely meant healed, right? That was to be the outcome. I was not going to face surgery or treatments. I was healed. The Scripture says, "By His stripes, I was healed." So, I am healed. Yes? I did everything right. I prayed, I called for the elders of the church, I claimed the scriptures. I did it right. Now, heal me!

But this was not the case for me. Surgery was booked. Doctors were calling several times a day. Pre-surgery, post-surgery, blood work, support groups . . . wait, I want off this ride. Can anyone hear me? I don't want to do any of these things. How come others get their healing and not me? Questions plagued my mind constantly. I was tormented by all the thoughts. And yet, I was continually trying to hold it together for the sake of others. It's like living in a constant theater performance.

"How are you doing?" I hate that question. Duh, I have a terrible, life-threatening disease. "Can I pray for you?" Sure, it hasn't worked so far, but go ahead." I was living with a mask on. I knew there were some in my family that couldn't handle the truth. What if, for just once, I spoke it? What if I told exactly how I felt? The humiliation of being undressed in front of people. Strangers standing over my body, touching and poking it, while claiming they were trying to help. The endless cycle of paperwork I had to fill out. And can we even talk about the financial struggle of cancer?

Depression climbed into my roller coaster car with me. It held my hand and wouldn't let go. It laughed at the first drop. When I thought I was going to fall out of the car, it pushed me. The ride was becoming just a blur, and my traveling companion was enjoying every minute of my fear.

Depression is not feeling down for an hour out of your day. It's not something to be underestimated. It's not beautiful at all; it's an ugly state of mind. Depression sets up a home in your life. It pulls up a chair. Depression puts you on the brink of tears because you can't find a shoe. It robs you of the desire to clean up; instead, you feel more like falling on the floor and crying. It taunts you, urging you not to brush your hair or your teeth for days at a time. After all, why should you? Depression makes you even forget when you ate last.

Depression is noticing how people start avoiding eye contact with you. They don't know how to proceed and engage in a conversation—so they avoid it. Cancer didn't erase me. I was still the same Elizabeth. But somehow, the disease changed how people viewed me. When I would see the look of pity in people's eyes, it would make me feel pity for myself. Then I would start to feel really sad (even more depressed), which is not good, because I did not want to feel that way.

I can remember one time having to explain my cancer history to a new doctor and he just acted normal. That was amazing. He continued the conversation, without his mouth dropping to the floor, and without making me feel like some sort of circus freak. He didn't ask me cancer questions. That was great. More of that would be nice. But unfortunately, most people are still afraid to even discuss cancer with you. Or they unknowingly ask the dumbest questions or offer the most ridiculous comments.

When depression is stalking you, it teams up with panic attacks—and they can hit you without warning—at work, at a birthday party, at a shopping mall, even at church, or in the car. My family would ask me, "Why are you crying? What's wrong?" And the only answer I could give was, "I have cancer, isn't that enough?" There were days where I'd roll out of bed and have black under my eyes from yesterday's mascara. It was there because I didn't have the energy to take my makeup off the night before.

My mom and husband would tell me that it would get better . . . and I would dream about when that might be. I felt nothing and everything all at once. Depression is not easy, nor is it a quick fix. It changes you. Appointment after appointment, I could hear the doctors talk, but it was as if I had gone deaf. I had turned into a zombie.

I met with a wig specialist . . . Depressing

I met with a breast prosthesis specialist . . . Depressing.

I met with a cancer therapist . . . Depressing.

I was given support group contacts . . . Depressing.

Would this ever stop? Once again, I want off this roller coaster ride!!!

When you are going through these emotions, it's as if you are the only one who has ever faced depression. No one could feel the way you do. But all through the Bible, you can read accounts of the giants of the faith who faced similar dark places in life. They all came out victoriously. Could God do that for me, too?

The Psalmist David was troubled and confessed to having deep depression. In many of the Psalms, he wrote of his sorrow, loneliness, fears, and guilt over his sins. David was a man full of sorrow and grief. And yet, David's honesty concerning his own failures and weaknesses gives us hope.

> *"My guilt has overwhelmed me like a burden too heavy to bear"* (Psalms 38:4 NIV).

> *"Why are you cast down, O my soul? And why are you disquieted within me? Hope in God; for I shall yet praise Him, the help of my countenance and my God"* (Psalms 42:11).

Cast down and disturbed is how he viewed himself. Overwhelmed with too much to bear was the way he felt. Yes, the beloved David, the man after God's own heart. He felt this ever-growing emotion. But he knew the key to overcoming was to keep calling on the name of the Lord. And he did so, constantly.

Consider the great prophet Elijah. He called down fire from heaven. He stopped the rain from falling for years. And yet, he was discouraged, weary, and afraid. After great spiritual victories over the prophets of Baal, this mighty man of God feared and ran for his life, fleeing from the threats of Jezebel. A woman brought him to the brink of utter despair. And there in the desert, he sat down. He gave up. He quit. He felt defeated and totally depressed. It is there that he prayed:

> *"It is enough . . . LORD, take my life"* (1 Kings 19:4).

"Wow! I have had enough!" During the course of your journey with cancer or other trials for that matter, you will probably make this statement many times. When you wake in the morning to face yet another treatment, "I have had enough." When your days are full of appointments, "I have had enough." When the pink gown doesn't cover your hiney, "I have definitely had enough."

Moving on to our dear friend, Jonah. He was angry and wanted to run away. Run away from the call of God on his life. Run away from his responsibilities. Run away from his purpose and destiny. There were days when I felt like this. I just wanted to run away and hide. I could die quietly in a hotel room somewhere. I could forget that I was sick and pretend that all was fine. But that is never the answer.

After God called Jonah to go to Nineveh to preach to the people, he ran away as far away as could. And after a storm at sea, being swallowed by a giant fish, and then being saved and given a second chance, he followed the call of God. He preached God's message to the people of Nineveh. God's mercy reached out to all people who turned to Him. But instead of rejoicing, Jonah got mad and said:

"Therefore now, O Lord, please take my life from me, for it is better for me to die than to live!" (Jonah 4:3)

I remember being in a service at a local church, the minister called his wife up. She began to give her testimony of being healed instantly from the very thing I had. What? I sat there trembling. The more she talked the more I wanted to run. I was angry. I was frustrated. Why her and not me? I should have rejoiced with her but no, I couldn't. I understand Jonah. He had spent days in a stinky, slimy belly of a great fish. How could he be happy for others? Is this attitude right? Of course not! But cancer is not right. And until you come to terms with your battle, it's easy to look at others with frustration and even with anger.

And even after God reached out to Jonah again with great compassion, he responded, *"It is right for me to be angry, even to death!"* (Jonah 4:9)

And let's not forget my man—Job! Everyone tells the great tale of Job.

He suffered through great loss, devastation, and physical illness. This righteous man of God lost literally everything. So great was his suffering and tragedy that even his own wife said, "Do you still hold fast to your integrity? Curse God and die?" (Job 2:9)

Sometimes, even your family will not understand why you are doing the things you are doing. They will turn from you because refusing to acknowledge the disease is easier. It is easier to pretend that nothing is going on. And at times, they will seem to get mad at you for being sick. You have to remember, they are struggling too. Cancer affects everyone around you. And you have to remind yourself, *They are in pain too. It's affected their lives just like it has yours.*

Though Job maintained his faithfulness to God through-out his life, he still struggled deeply through the trenches of pain:

"Why did I not die at birth? Why did I not perish when I came from the womb?" (Job 3:11)

"I am not at ease, nor am I quiet; I have no rest, for trouble comes" (Job 3:26).

"My soul loathes my life; I will give free course to my com-plaint, I will speak in the bitterness of my soul" (Job 10:1).

"Terrors are turned upon me; they pursue my honor as the wind, and my prosperity has passed like a cloud. And now my soul is poured out because of my plight; the days of affliction take hold of me. My bones are pierced in me at night, and my gnawing pains take no rest" (Job 30:15-17).

Wow! Have I depressed you yet? So, you feel like run-ning and hiding from me. Maybe you would like to return my book to the bookstore. Depression comes. But it doesn't have to stay. With all these examples, they picked themselves up and went on. They didn't give in to depression. No, they kicked it out of the car (well, in that day, they would have to kick it out of the cart, the wagon, or the chariot).

I would be in the wrong if I didn't share the greatest story of overcoming depression that I know. And it truly is a faith-building lesson for us all.

Even Jesus Himself was deeply tormented by what lay before Him. He had a moment of overwhelming fear and frustration.

He knew what was to come. He knew that God had called him to a journey of great suffering; He knew what must happen in order for all of us to live truly free. Our Savior was willing to pay the price on our behalf, but it wasn't an easy road. When you think about it, it's really profound. Jesus knew His future. He knew the impending pain, loneliness, and death. Isaiah prophesied that Christ would be "a man of sorrows and acquainted with grief" (Isaiah 53:3).

Jesus had read these scriptures. He knew they were about *His* journey.

We can be assured that whatever we face, Jesus understands our weakness and suffering, our greatest times of trouble and despair, because He, too, traveled that road. In the garden, through the night, Jesus prayed—all alone—calling out to His Father, asking Him if there could just be another way. He even confessed to His followers:

"My soul is exceedingly sorrowful, even to death. Stay here and watch." He went a little farther, and fell on the ground, and prayed that if it were possible, the hour might pass from Him. And He said, "Abba, Father, all things are possible for You. Take this cup away from Me; nevertheless, not what I will, but what You will" (Mark 14:34-36).

The Word says that so great was His pain, "His sweat became like great drops of blood falling down to the ground." (Luke 22:44)

He was depressed. He felt alone. He was in anguish. But that's why He understands just what we are going through. He is on the ride with us. We are not alone.

David, Elijah, Jonah, Job, and Jesus, I think my roller coaster cars are full. I am in excellent company. They faced this horrible emotion head on. And they conquered it. So I can be of good courage, and you can too.

David became a great King.

Elijah went to heaven in a chariot of fire.

Jonah changed a nation.

Job was restored to everything he lost and more.

And come on . . . Jesus was resurrected and sits on the right hand of God.

What is true about all these stories and many others is this: God was with them. Close. Nearby. He never left them. You may feel like He did, but trust me, He is close at hand.

"The Lord is near to those who have a broken heart, and saves such as have a contrite spirit" (Psalms 34:18).

God was there in the good days and in the dark days, too. He did not condemn them for their questions and pain. He didn't tell them to just tough it out. He also did not tell them it would be alright. He reached down to their deepest pit of suffering and lifted them out. That is what God does. He will lift us up out of the miry clay and set our feet on a rock.

And He is still doing the same for His people now. When we least expect it, He will show up. He will take care of us.

The day of my first surgery, I was sitting on the side of our bed in a very low place emotionally. They had informed me that they would keep cutting till we had clear margins. I had no idea what would be left after they finished. That was frightening. I was preparing myself for whatever may come. It takes preparation of spirit to face a major surgery. And that is exactly what I was trying to do. I still couldn't come to grips with the fact that I wasn't healed. I felt like maybe God had forgotten me. The tumor was large and growing. It had started causing a lot of pain. And the pain and fear were taking a toll on me mentally. I was struggling.

So, I was sitting there, feeling devastated and deserted. My mom had the television blasting louder than necessary with preachers quoting scriptures and singing songs of deliverance. Mike was packing clothes and praying in the Spirit. And I was doing nothing. My feet were dangling off the side of the bed. It was like a dream. People were talking. I wasn't listening. They were asking questions. I wasn't answering. I just wanted to crawl up on the bed and be left alone. My mind was running like a racehorse.

Why wasn't I healed? Why didn't God touch me? Why do others get healed? Does God exist? Why didn't the formula for prayerful success work for me? Am I reprobate? Is it because I did something wrong? Questions abounded.

Mike was helping me put on my shoes. The television was so loud. I told my mom, "Please turn that off. I don't even like that preacher." I lie not. At that exact moment in time (and I get chills when I think about it) the preacher yelled through the television, "Don't turn me off." We all froze. What did he say? Again, he yelled, "Don't touch that remote. There is a lady sitting on the side of her bed. You are facing major surgery. You don't even like me. But God is going to use me to build your faith. God is going to touch you. You are going to know that He hasn't forsaken you. That tumor is reducing in size."

It was as if time stood still. We were in slow motion. I wish you could have been in the room. Our eyes were so big. We were afraid to talk, afraid that the preacher would yell at us again. My mom immediately started doing a victory dance. Mike said, "Did you hear that?" We were shocked. I didn't know what God was doing for me, but I realized He had not forsaken me and He was speaking to me. True to the word of the Lord, the tumor shrunk. Strangely, it did not disappear. (Why didn't God do that?) But it reduced in size at least 50%. I don't think I will ever understand that part of it, but I'm thankful, because surgery was not as invasive as it would have been otherwise.

And in that moment, total healing wasn't my top priority. My highest aspiration was allowing God to be God in this storm and asking Him to use me any way He saw fit. It was about accepting my role in this dark place and knowing that God was going to bring light to me and shine light through me. I realized that I was still headed for surgery, but maybe, just maybe, God had a bigger plan for me. He sent a preacher to yell at me from a television set and it knocked the life out of that tumor.

The greatest truth that I was learning was this: we have a Savior who understands our pain, who knows about every weakness and hurt, and reaches out with compassion and hope.

He is Healer. Redeemer. Restorer. And Friend.

And maybe the healing wasn't going to come to me the way I expected it. Maybe I was going to grow in this storm. Maybe my faith would reach a higher peak.

He will never waste the seasons of suffering we face, but He will use them, in some way, to bring good, to instill purpose, to help others, and to make us stronger.

I was going to be made stronger. I was going to grow in this storm. I was going to be the heroine in my story and not the victim. And now, I was ready. I felt like the serpent was already being bruised under my feet.

Overcoming Depression Scriptures

Psalms 34:17

The righteous cry out, and the LORD hears, and delivers them out of all their troubles.

1 Peter 5:7

Casting all your care upon Him, for He cares for you.

Isaiah 41:10

"Fear not, for I am with you; be not dismayed, for I am your God. I will strengthen you, yes, I will help you, I will uphold you with My righteous right hand."

Jeremiah 29:11 (KJV)

"For I know the thoughts that I think toward you, saith the LORD, thoughts of peace, and not of evil, to give you an expected end."

Proverbs 12:25 (MKJV)

Heaviness in the heart of man makes it stoop, but a good word makes it glad.

Psalms 9:9

The LORD also will be a refuge for the oppressed, a refuge in times of trouble.

2 Timothy 1:7

For God has not given us a spirit of fear, but of power and of love and of a sound mind.

John 10:10

"The thief does not come except to steal, and to kill, and to destroy. I have come that they may have life, and that they may have it more abundantly."

Overcoming Depression Quotes

"The only thing more exhausting than being depressed is pretending that you're not."—Anonymous

"That's the thing about depression: A human being can survive almost anything, as long as she sees the end in sight. But depression is so insidious, and it compounds daily, that it's impossible to ever see the end. The fog is like a cage without a key."—Elizabeth Wurtzel

"The pupil dilates in darkness and in the end finds light, just as the soul dilates in misfortune and in the end finds God." —Victor Hugo

"There are times when explanations, no matter how reasonable, just don't seem to help." —Fred Rogers

"Depression lies. It tells you you've always felt this way, and you always will. But you haven't, and you won't." —Halley Cornell

"You can't stay in your corner of the forest waiting for others to come to you. You have to go to them sometimes." —Winnie the Pooh

"Just when the caterpillar thought the world was over, it became a butterfly."—Anonymous

"There are moments when I wish I could roll back the clock and take all the sadness away, but I have the feeling that if I did, the joy would be gone as well." —Nicholas Sparks

"Never lose hope. This life is worth the struggle. Your future self is pleading with you to stay. You are more than your thoughts. You are more than your fears and stronger than you give yourself credit for. You can be an overcomer." —Elizabeth Shreve

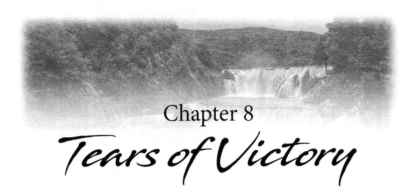

Chapter 8
Tears of Victory

How do we define the word victory? According to the dictionary, it is the state of having conquered in a battle or a contest, having overcome an enemy or an antagonist. It means conquering something or someone. That sounds fantastic. But to a survivor or a recovered patient, the word takes on a whole new meaning. Victory is feeling like yourself again. It is being able to talk about anything else but the sickness. It is having a week of not being surrounded by doctors' appointments, scans, and blood work. Victory is letting the word cancer fade into the background. It means taking back your life.

Cancer causes you to have an identity crisis. Somewhere in the journey, you lose yourself. All your hopes, dreams, and passions are put in the background. In the forefront is the disease; it takes up all your time, energy, and life. There are two periods of time in cancer: before your diagnosis and after your diagnosis. So much of your life revolves around the disease. All the people in your life get drawn into your never-ending saga. Pre-cancer you had a life. You knew where you were headed. Cancer came in and changed the script. You were the leading lady and now you are just an extra. Everything is controlled by that horrible word, cancer (notice, I am not capitalizing the word now). In the crosshairs of the struggle, people whisper and try not to

> Cancer causes you to have an identity crisis. Somewhere in the journey, you lose yourself.

make you feel bad. Your children use phrases like, "If you feel up to it" or "We don't have to go." Victory for a survivor is finding your new normal. You have to find *you* again, whoever and whatever that may be. This is my definition of victory (even though you won't find it in the dictionary).

Slowly but surely, conversations with people will have nothing to do with cancer. It won't be the first thing you think of in the morning. Cancer was once my life 24/7; it was what I thought about all the time (even when I was asleep, I had nightmares about it). It was really hard to focus on anything else, or to feel like anything else was really that important. Because it wasn't. It is a war, and you are in the position as General (underneath the Commanding General who lends you His authority). You have to continually be planning strategies and countermoves. Victory is being able to relax. The enemy surrenders and the dust of battle settles.

I wish I could say it's all behind me, that I've moved on and thoughts of cancer never even cross my mind, but that would be a big, big lie. I worry about it far less than I did, but the fear and anxiety are still there. Every time I read or hear of another person whose cancer has returned, or who has passed away, I remember, "Oh yeah, that could be me." When I have a pain, my mind says, "There it is again." Believe me, with each pain for a while, I would call the doctor. I even had a scan to just put my mind at ease. But right there—hiding and peaking out from behind the curtain—is the recurring thought, *It has returned*. That battle of the mind is always there. Maybe this is it. Maybe that, maybe, maybe . . . It's a never-ending struggle. So, victory to me is going one day without the thought that it's back. Now that really *is* victory.

I do not, in any way, believe that cancer is a good thing. No one should have to face it. It is not a blessing. It is definitely not something God puts on you. It stinks. I do not recommend it. It gets a zero-star rating on Yelp. But I will say that cancer has taught me some important lessons. So, hear a few of my victory lessons.

Victory came in the form of making new friends. The door to many lasting and warm relationships happened during my time at the oncology center. I have had some amazing people come into my life, who I probably never would have met if not for having cancer. Some of these people had cancer and some didn't, but they have all been connected to me through the whole cancer 'thingy.' Developing new friendships is always a good thing, and maintaining those friendships is an even better thing. Until my diagnosis, my friendship circle consisted mostly of people in the ministry. In the words of the movie, "Aladdin," I began experiencing, "A Whole New World."

Victory manifested when God used me to encourage others. You spend a lot of time sitting in waiting rooms, treatment areas, and refreshment queues. I used this time to share my faith, my sadness, and my goals. The people with whom you share your journey become your family and you become part of theirs. You spend hours, days, and months with them. You are with them during their most vulnerable times. Deciding to be there for others helped me through it. One day, I walked into the check-in area. A sweet lady jumped up and ran toward me. She said, "We've been waiting on you. Please come over and brighten our day." God has given me a gift to bring laughter and joy to others. This gift expanded by leaps and bounds during this time. You learn when to laugh and when to cry with those who are suffering. Sharing scriptures with those hurting, and watching it wash over their troubled souls is victory. I often wondered why I had to go through this trial, but during those times of talking, I realized God was with me and He had a purpose. But I have often thought, *Next time, God, if You don't mind, let me share at a ballgame or birthday party. If it be possible, can we pass over the oncology ward?*

Victory is being able to distinguish between true friends and those who really are not. Cancer allowed me to learn who the real friends were in my life. True friends are those who come into your life, seeing the most negative part of you, but are not ready to leave you, even though you can't offer them anything in return. It is a one-way relationship during a crisis like that. And yet, these loyal ones make a conscious choice to stay by your side. You need them. Your support system is crucial during challenging times like this. Surrounding your-self with strong, prayerful people will help the journey go smoother. Although this has a painful, opposite side (learn-ing which friends weren't as great as you thought), it's still a really nice up-side when you see faithful commitment and compassion from amazing people who rally to your cause. Some people I thought would always be by my side left so fast my head was spinning. They couldn't look at me unless it was the look that no cancer patient ever wants or needs (pity or sadness). Believe me, you are better off without this kind of friend. It hurts. When they stay away, they are really doing you a favor.

I remember one day when the going was really rough. I had cried for hours. All I could say was, "Am I going to die?" My mom brought in the mail. There was a beautiful card from a wonderful friend who lived many miles away. It was exactly what I needed. The words inside calmed my spirit. She will never know what that card did for me that day. It was a simple act of kindness that lifted me out of a very dark place. That is the kind of friend I want to be. Cancer will definitely strength-en your most valuable relationships and there are certain people of whom I can now say confidently, "They will be my friends for life." But it also allowed me to have the courage to back away from those who left me stranded in my dilemma.

Victory is learning to appreciate everything. And I mean everything. I think I already had quite a lot of appreciation for most things pre-cancer, but my gratitude intensified in a major way during the journey and especially afterward. I see beauty in new ways and I value every minute of existence— in a way I think most people don't. A life-threatening disease is like an alarm clock. You wake up to all the things you've been asleep to—and you capture in your viewfinder what previously was often overlooked.

You realize that work is not everything. Relationships take center stage. You want to go on vacations, laugh, and make memories. You want to fulfill your calling. You want your children to remember you in a warm, endearing way. Fear and intimidation that stopped you before seem so small compared to cancer. I still have times when something reminds me of my battle, and I feel tears well up in my eyes, because I am just so overwhelmed with thankfulness that I am still alive. Alive is an AWESOME word. I feel very, very blessed every day. I am favored beyond measure. I begged God to let me live and here I am. Alive. Living life to its fullness is my goal. Every day is another victory.

Victory is walking through new doors. I think it's a pretty common sequence of events, to go through something hard/awful/challenging and then realize that the battle has actually pushed you in a positive direction. Cancer changes you, but cancer is not the door. Jesus says, "Walk on it" and your enemy becomes ashes under the soles of your feet. But you look up, and there Jesus is, standing, radiating His glory and saying, "I am the door"—the door of opportunity, the door of purpose, the door of wisdom, the door of genuine love, and a host of other things. If you allow it, putting the "C" problem under your feet and walking toward the Lord will change you for the better. It will make you fearless. He promises, "I open and no one can shut." He is there, not just one door, but a series of doors—leading to better things than you could have imagined.

There is so much I can say about being victorious. It has been an ongoing journey for me. In everything we do, there has to be a strong desire to walk in victory. I am reminded of so many in the Bible who had to overcome.

God loves an underdog. He loves to take the most unlikely person to become the hero or heroine in some tense drama and then He shows that person how to win with His wisdom. That man, woman, boy, or girl then becomes the person no one ever thought could be victorious. God makes that unlikely candidate for greatness, the victor that others look to for help. My man, Gideon, is a perfect example of the underdog. God often chooses those for whom the world has little or no expectations. He does that so He alone can receive the glory that He rightfully deserves.

> God loves an underdog. He loves to take the most unlikely person to become the hero or heroine in some tense drama.

When the angel of the Lord came to Gideon and said, "The Lord is with you, O mighty man of valor," the Midianites were oppressing God's chosen people (Judges 6:12 ESV). Every time the harvest was ripe, the enemy would sweep down out of the mountains and raid the countryside, stripping away all of the harvest and stealing the livestock. "So Israel was greatly impoverished because of the Midianites and the children of Israel cried out to the LORD" (Judges 6:7).

But the Angel of the Lord told Gideon, "Go in this might of yours and save Israel from the hand of the Midianites. Have not I sent you?" Gideon had already argued, "O my Lord, how can I save Israel? Indeed my clan is the weakest in Manasseh, and I am the least in my father's house." (Judges 6:15). But God didn't listen, or at least, He didn't accept those words of self-degradation. Wow, I think I must have told God similar things many times. "Who me? I don't think so, Lord. Don't you realize I am nothing?"

Here is why this Bible story is so hopeful and helpful to us. Gideon was the least of his clan, he was the runt of the litter (so to speak). This is what my daddy always called Mike (because my daddy was about 6'4" and Mike is only 5'8" and a half—Mike always likes to include that final half-an-inch). There are many times that I have felt like the least of everyone around me. Gideon was hiding from the Midianites when the Angel of the Lord approached him and yet he described him as a "mighty man of valor" and told him, "Go in this might of yours" (Judges 6:14). You have to wonder if Gideon looked over his shoulder and thought, *Does He really mean me?* There are definitely times that the Lord and I have played "hide and seek."

The point is this: God sees what will be before it even exists. He knows the future and speaks as if it's already present, because, with God, it really is! God knew that Gideon's tiny little force of 300 farmers and shepherds could never destroy a camp of 135,000 seasoned, experienced, and well-trained Midianites soldiers. But with God, all things are possible. So don't ever lose hope, even if the odds look exceedingly hopeless. Even when the doctor reports come back negative, even when you have absolutely no energy, even when things are going poorly, don't ever cave in. They would later say of Gideon, "God has given into his hand Midian and all the camp." I am proof that God will give you victory. It doesn't matter how small, insignificant, or powerless you imagine yourself to be. God steps in and lifts you to heights you never knew possible.

Victory is realizing that the battle has been, and is always, the Lord's. Yes, you have been the instrument in His hands. Others have helped. But He is the One who guided your steps and ordered your paths. I didn't believe I would be victorious in the beginning. I didn't even know if I would survive. God still helped me overcome. And he will do the same for you.

Victory is "ringing the bell." Why is this tradition so meaningful to those who overcome cancer? It's symbolic. There was a big brass bell hanging in the cancer treatment center I frequented, and next to it, a poem. The "victorious one" who finishes treatments is supposed to read the following poem out loud, then ring the bell:

> *"Ringing out*
> *Ring this bell*
> *Three times well*
> *Its toll to clearly say,*

My treatment is done
This course is run
And I am on my way!"

How did it start? An admiral in the U.S. Navy, Irve Le Moyne, was undergoing radiation therapy for head and neck cancer and told his doctor that he planned to follow a Navy tradition of ringing a bell to signify when the job was done. He brought a brass bell to his last treatment, rang it several times, and left it as a donation. It was mounted on a wall plaque in the Main Building's Radiation Treatment Center with the above poem. It has become a symbol of victory.

For me, ringing the bell was an important milestone and celebratory moment in my cancer journey. The hospital staff was happy to gather together with me and my family and friends to celebrate and applaud the ringing of the bell.

It was pure joy for us. There were hugs and smiles and tears. For me, it meant that I had won round one of the fight, knocking out my opponent, and hopefully that would be the only round I would ever have to face. It was done.

I remember the whole day like it was yesterday. Treatments were about to be over. That day would be the last day of undressing and laying on that long steel table. It would be the last day I would hold back tears as the machine wrapped around me. It would be the last day I would listen for that clicking buzzing sound, the sound of radiation being shot into me. Unless you have faced this, you cannot relate. I can tell you about it, but words are insufficient.

I had told the whole staff that on my last day, a party was in order. And I wasn't talking about something on a small scale. When we arrived, a spread of delicious food and drinks were on a long table. I had picked up confetti shooters, balloons, and noise makers. When you know that a trial is almost over, you celebrate. It is seeing the light at the end of a long and dark tunnel. One of the things that kept me going was envisioning myself ringing that bell and my family being around me and being so happy to be done. I think having something like that in mind helped me get through it.

> One of the things that kept me going was envisioning myself ringing that bell and my family being around me and being so happy to be done.

I had a boombox with me that day so we could play an old disco song called, "Ring My Bell." It was a dance song. And boy, did we dance. I even saw Mike doing a little dance out of the corner of my eye. We shot the confetti, let the balloons float up to the ceiling . . . and we made so much noise. All my staff friends gathered around. My family and my best friends were there. Two of my doctors showed their faces. It was a time of rejoicing. It was a victory.

Over and over we all sang the line, "*You can ring my bell (ring my bell, ding, dong, ding).*" Jubilation, yes! But it was more than that; it was a serious proclamation, a prophetic declaration in the Spirit, even using a secular song.

So, what is victory? It is winning. It is making it to the finish line. But I think most of all, it is having people in your life that walk with you through dark places to get there. It is knowing you are not alone. It is believing that God will never leave you nor forsake you. Victory will bring tears to your eyes—but they are a different kind. They are tears of praise and gratitude, because you are just so grateful to be among the living.

Tomorrow is holding something beautiful for you. Hold on to that hope and get ready to celebrate. Rejoice evermore. Ring that bell in your heart long before you hear it with your ears—and you will.

Victory Scriptures

Deuteronomy 20:4

"For the LORD your God is He who goes with you, to fight for you against your enemies, to save you."

Philippians 4:13

I can do all things through Christ who strengthens me.

John 16:33

"These things I have spoken to you, that in Me you may have peace. In the world you will have tribulation; but be of good cheer, I have overcome the world."

1 Corinthians 15:57

But thanks be to God, who gives us the victory through our Lord Jesus Christ.

Ephesians 6:13

Therefore take up the whole armor of God, that you may be able to withstand in the evil day, and having done all, to stand.

Ephesians 6:10

Finally, my brethren, be strong in the Lord, and in the power of his might.

2 Corinthians 12:9

And He said to me, "My grace is sufficient for you, for My strength is made perfect in weakness." Therefore most gladly I will rather boast in my infirmities, that the power of Christ may rest upon me.

1 John 5:4

For whatever is born of God overcomes the world. And this is the victory that has overcome the world—our faith.

Victory Quotes

"You cannot expect victory and plan for defeat."
—Joel Osteen

"Don't let mental blocks control you. Set yourself free. Confront your fear and turn the mental blocks into building blocks." —Dr. Roopleen

"The fight isn't over until you win." —Robin Hobb

"Great victory requires great risk." —Hera

"Who you are tomorrow begins with what you do today." —Tim Fargo

"I am not a victim. No matter what I have been through, I'm still here. I have a history of victory." —Steve Maraboli

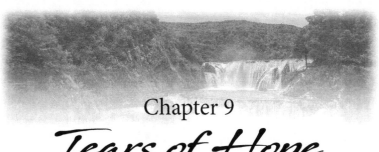

Chapter 9
Tears of Hope

So here we are, getting close to the end of this book. Just one more chapter after this for me to pour out my heart, and then the epilogue. This chapter is one of my favorites. It's a good chapter, "Tears of Hope." Hope is the belief that a positive outcome lies ahead. This belief can be difficult to hold onto in the face of cancer. Knowing how to create a sense of hope in your life can help you become a cancer survivor with strength and confidence or any other kind of "survivor" you need to be.

There is no right or wrong path to finding hope. Hope comes easy for some. Others may not be sure how to hold onto that feeling during some intimidating or overwhelming experiences. We all hope for different things at different times in our lives. When I was first diagnosed with cancer, all I could hope for was that treatment would be successful and that the cancer would go into remission. I relied on hope to get me through the difficult days of diagnosis and treatment and the changes that were happening in my life. And there are many changes that will happen. Even to this day, I am changing. I am learning to walk in my role as a survivor—confident and strong.

One of the first changes is the uncertainty of life. Unfortunately, I am still prone to panicking over every new pain/bump/mole/anomaly that presents itself to me. I still have this unsettled feeling that a bomb is about to go off. Every time I learn of a person who has a reoccurrence, the world stops, and I am crushed by the weight of impending death. That could be me. I could be dead in a few years. The thoughts rattle my brain—*Don't get comfortable because this could all end soon. You know it always returns.* It is a constant voice in my head. That is why hope is so important. Mike has a quote that I love, "Without Christ, life is a hopeless end, but with Christ, life is endless hope." It is something you must cling to. Hold onto it like Indian Jones tenaciously gripped his whip. Surround yourself with hopeful people. This is so important.

My back hurts. Was that pain there before? No, that's a new pain. Hope.

Is that a lump? Touch, feel, and examine. Hope.

My mind will never find peace from this torment. Hope.

It will return and take me out. Hope.

You must always let hope come to your rescue.

Sometimes I get exhausted from hoping. I get tired of having to talk to myself and encourage myself. In times like that I turn to the Word of God. In Him, I find what I need. Here is a good promise: Romans 15:13 –" Now may the God of hope fill you with all joy and peace in believing, that you may abound in hope by the power of the Holy Spirit."

Emotions can override everything. They can quickly cause the collapse of logic and reason. They will carry you down a rabbit hole of disbelief. You will soon discover you are lost, unless you allow hope to be your guide.

Guilt is the enemy of hope. Can we talk about the feeling of guilt? Guilt will steal away your hope. Guilt—because everything is actually, really great right now and none of my fears have become a reality. Guilt—because I know people who are not so fortunate and would trade places with me in a second. Guilt—for feeling like I'm not doing enough with whatever extra years I have been given. Guilt—that I am not hoping enough.

One thing that has helped me overcome the guilt, emotionally and mentally, in being a survivor is being able to talk to other people about my experience and listen to them about their experience. I am able to spread hope in their lives—and while I am doing it for them, it happens fresh for me all over again.

This is a powerful tool in your recovery kit. You must share your story. You must be raw and honest. Don't ever candy-coat the journey through this or any other major disease. Cancer is a horrible thing. But you can wrap up the bitter reality with hope. Instead of leaving a foul smell of defeat in people's lives, we must leave the sweet fragrance of hope.

Hope is flexible and changes as you go through experiences. Only you will know what works best for you. It is very important to learn this lesson. What works for others may not work for you. We all have different personalities. We all have different lines of logic and ways of working through things in our minds. Having hope links your past and present to the future. You have a vision for what you hope will happen. Whether it does or not, just envisioning it can make you feel better. Hope means understanding that your past cannot limit your future.

The word "hope" is found 142 times in the King James Version of the Bible. The first time you see hope, it is in the book of Ruth. In chapter 1 verse 12, Naomi (Ruth's mother-in-law), claimed that she had no hope. That's right, she actually confessed that she had no hope. That is a terrible place to be: the place of "no hope." In the beginning of any trial there is often a season of "no hope," the season when your mind can't come to grips with the why, the what, the when, and the how concerning all of the things that are happening to you. It is a time when the world seems to be caving in on you.

> The word "hope" is found 142 times in the King James Version of the Bible.

Naomi's Tragedy and Her Response

Tragedy (like cancer or any other illness) will do one of two things to you. It will either move you closer to God or further away from Him. Naomi was a strong woman, who instead of being humbled, became bitter and resentful. She even changed her name to Mara meaning bitter. Before we start throwing rocks at Naomi (Mara), you need to try and put yourself in her shoes. Over a period of time, she lost her husband, then her two sons. Why would God put her in such a place? I must have asked myself this a thousand times between my diagnosis and now . . . Why God? How come? God, where are you in all of this?

I am sure Naomi's mind was flooded with memories—the time she left her homeland to follow her husband, her boys growing up strong and happy in front of her eyes, and even all the times she had worshipped God when her life wasn't the easiest path to walk.

Familiar? After the dark curtain fell on Act One, it was lifted again for Act Two—but the stage was empty except for her and her two daughters-in-law. She felt abandoned by God, alone, and afraid. Haven't you felt this way at times? Those are two the most recurring emotions that I suffered (feeling abandoned and afraid). It is during those times that you cannot forget the promises of God. First Peter 1:13 says, "Wherefore gird up the loins of your mind, be sober, and hope to the end for the grace that is to be brought unto you at the revelation of Jesus Christ." (KJV)

> It is easy to forget God's promises, if you allow yourself to sink into the quicksand of despair.

It is easy to forget God's promises, if you allow yourself to sink into the quicksand of despair. The more you struggle, the deeper you go. Emotions run wild when you're desperate. When you're hacking your way through jungle underbrush, it's hard to find the promise path. You have to bring every negative thought into captivity and whatever you do, get back on the path. I had to constantly take control of my thinking. I could feel bitterness trying to overtake me—almost every day.

The next stop on Naomi's journey was anger. She got upset with God and questioned the Most High's plans. When she and her family fled the famine in Judah, I'm sure she was convinced it was the Lord's answer for them all. But who did she blame for all the painful circumstances that had evolved since then? Of course, the God who she had originally praised. She dared to declare, "The Almighty has dealt very bitterly with me" (Ruth 1:20). Okay, you may not want to admit it. But you have been angry a time or two. I confess to you, anger was one of my responses. I was angry that I was sick. I was angry that God didn't heal me as soon as I believed. I was even angry at times that He had healed others and not me. Yep, I admit it, I was angry.

Naomi's present troubles caused her to lose her past vision, her purpose, and her faith in God's love. Hope had to be reborn. I am so thankful for that moment when I first experienced the rebirth of hope. Troubles will test our patience. They will cause us to lose our way. Often, we will blame God for every bad thing that happens! But if we open our hearts, let hope guide us, and refuse to become bitter, we can more easily comprehend how today's problems are truly leading us to tomorrow's answers. In other words, whenever faith in God looks to the future, it becomes hope. And whenever hope rests on the Word of God, it becomes faith. Hope and Faith are closely related that way and are often found working together.

After the death of her husband and sons, Naomi made the decision to return to Bethlehem (which means "the house of bread"). When we go through difficulties we can't seem to solve, or hard places out of which we see no escape, it's not unusual to just give up, pull away from others, and even draw back from God. Naomi was ready to return and claim any inheritance left by her husband's death. One of her husband's relatives would need to step up to the plate and take responsibility for her care. This is called the law of the "kinsman redeemer" (a provision in the Old Testament). Naomi was a woman without hope. She was carrying the heavy burden of bitterness. But she knew if she returned, it was possible that a solution could be found.

Too often, when we are hurt by sickness, disappointment, or betrayal, we can't see ourselves rising above our pain. That may be because we have more faith in the power of where we came from than in the potential of where we are going. Open your eyes and realize that hope is always set on the future.

One of Naomi's daughters-in-law, Orpah, decided to remain in Moab. In essence, her choice was to "live in the past." Moab is a place of bad experiences and memories. In Moab, you're always caught in the web of yesterday. It's the "If I had just done this, or that" land. It's a place that kills hope like a spider devouring its vulnerable prey. Linger in your "Moab," and you will constantly be found rehearsing your former failures, and all the times you felt like God abandoned you. You will constantly relive events in your past you'd rather forget (in my case, appointments and treatments).

To travel into the future blessings God has in store for you, you must make your break from Moab! You must always be "forgetting those things which are behind and reaching forward to those things which are ahead" (Philippians 3:13). This is one of my favorite scriptures of all times. You must be like Ruth. Even when Naomi was blaming God for all their sorrow, Ruth said, "Your God will be my God." She didn't run from the source of hope, but she ran to hope. Hope was guiding her to her future. Neither of them ever knew the greatness of what was unfolding.

> To travel into the future blessings God has in store for you, you must make your break from Moab!

Ruth eventually married Boaz, and and she bore him a son named Obed, who became the father of Jesse, who became the father of King David. And of course, the line of David ultimately brought forth that blessed One called "the Son of David"—Jesus (Yeshua) the Messiah, who eventually brought salvation to the whole world. So you never know where pain and sorrow are leading—it may be a place that is far greater than anything you could have imagined.

It takes faith to leave your past and head toward your future! I'm sure we all know people who have remained in their "Moab." Whether it was a failed marriage, a devastating sickness, or the death of a loved one, they talk about it as if it just happened—no matter how much time has passed! They're trapped in the pit of bitterness, and they are paralyzed, angry, and lonely, even when they're in a crowd. They're not drawn to help others—their faith is bruised, and they live in a constant state of despair. It's not a place you want to call home!

I have dwelled in Moab. Have you? Truthfully, I spent months living in that bitter land. My treatments were over. It seemed all things were working out for my good. But my mind could not *hope* that it was over. Constantly, I would ask Mike, "Do you think it will return." To all my doctors, "When do you think I'll be sick again." I hated all the pink ribbons. It was just a reminder of the pain of the past.

One of the reasons, it has taken me so long to write this book is this: I just didn't want to face it again in my mind. With each word on the page, I felt like I was being dragged back into that pit of despair. I was sitting at a coffee shop writing, but I was really in Moab. So, I would stop and start. Mike would encourage me to write. I would get angry because he had no idea how hard it was for me to relive my fears. Worst of all, I was afraid to talk about hope because if it came back, the book would be a lie. My "Moab" seemed to always conquer my "Bethlehem."

When I finally started feeling like a conqueror something would happen to jerk the rug out from under me. The last time I tried to finish this book, we were in a meeting. Mike had me come up to the stage to tell of God's greatness in this storm I had faced. I was hopeful. After speaking, I knew it. I had finally won the battle of my mind. Those words would never sprint in my spirit again, *It will come back.* Afterward, a lady came up to me. Remember, the battle had been raging inside of me about a recurrence happening. She was smiling and talking about her sister having cancer.

Smiling back, I made the mistake of asking how long she was out (it's a phrase meaning, "How long has it been in remission?"). Her smile disappeared and she spoke these hair-raising words. "Oh, my sister is dead. The cancer came back with a vengeance." The definition of that word is punishment inflicted or retribution. It was as if she had tattooed that word on my mind and I couldn't remove the tattoo. The ink was indelible: "Vengeance, vengeance, vengeance"—it loomed before me and the sound of the word echoed over and over in my head and heart.

It sent me into a whirlwind of crazy. I lost all hope of a future. I believed that it was inevitable. It was over. Cancer would take its vengeance. Obsessing with self-check started happening again. I would give myself an exam all through the day. Feeling for a lump, looking for a mole, or living in fear when I forgot something, became an unavoidable replay every day (like the needle on a scratched record going back to the same part of the song over and over). The lady had no idea what she did to me. She put me on a caravan to Moab. And there, it seemed, I was doomed to stay. Mike couldn't help me. My mom tried to rescue me. I shut down, emotionally, mentally, and even physically. The doctor reassured me that I was in the low percentile of recurrence. Even that didn't bring me hope.

Trash Became Treasure

I still attended Mike's meetings. I still smiled and pretended everything was fine. It is amazing that people often are not sensitve to the pain of others. I don't think, beside Mike, that anyone was aware of my thoughts. Where was God? Where was hope? Hope had left the building. I didn't go to the stage anymore. I refused to talk of hope. I was waiting and watching for vengeance. Moab was my address now.

Then—once again—something really miraculous happened. It was a night like any other night. The worship music was playing. People were singing and dancing. The ministers were on the stage. The atmosphere was full of happiness and hopefulness. And I was sitting on the back row lost in my torment. So heavy was my heart that I thought I could faint. Would Mike remarry? Would my children remember? Did I do anything in my life worth remembering? So many questions and no answers to be found. Like I said, a night just like all my other nights.

But that night was destined to be different.

Someone touched me on my arm. I didn't want to be bothered. She was short with grey hair. I thought to myself, *Lady you are barking up the wrong tree.* If she wanted prayer, I was not the person to come to. Advice, I didn't have any. Or at least, none that a minister's wife should have. She was persistent. I feel bad about it now, but I wanted her to go away. Leave me alone, lady! I brushed her off again. But she would not budge.

She reached out to me and handed me what looked like a dirty napkin. She whispered in my ear, "Don't look at this till you get to where you are staying." Great, she wants me to throw her trash away. And then she left. Great! Now, I am not only fighting sickness, but I've been demoted to the position of being a janitor.

The service felt like it went on for hours. I was exhausted and ready to go. When you are in a storm, the happiness of everyone else just infuriates you. And the fact that it feels like no one cares you are dying inside makes it even worse. You believe people should see through your mask. It looks like all the discerning ministers would see you are slowly losing it. It's like a mental suicide going on right in front of them. But no one can see it.

Finally, we got back to the room. Mike picked up 'the gift' (the dirty-napkin-looking-thingy from the older lady) asking what it was. I really didn't care. I had tossed it on the counter when we got back. I picked it up and looked. Hmmm. There was a scripture reference written inside the napkin (just the chapter and verse). So, it wasn't trash after all. But once again, I wasn't that interested. Mike convinced me to get a Bible and find the scripture. I was at my wit's end. Vengeance! No Hope! No future! Echoing in my mind day and night.

There it was—Nahum. *Who is Nahum?* I thought. Oh, he's a minor prophet. Great, my scripture comes from the minor league. But because I love my husband, I picked up my Bible—not because I believed it was important, and not because I had faith, and definitely, not because I had any hope. But because I love him so much, I agreed to look.

Do you know how hard it is to find Nahum? Finally, after flipping back and forth, I found it and looked again for the verse.

Nahum 1:9 (KJV) was the verse scribbled on that dirty napkin.

Okay, what's it gonna say, I thought—with no expectation or excitement whatsoever.

I looked down at the Bible and started reading. Amazed. I felt the prophetic anointing embrace and envelop me as I silently mouthed the words:

"What do ye imagine against the Lord? He will make an utter end: affliction shall not rise up the second time."

Freeze! What? I read it again . . .

"What do ye imagine against the Lord? He will make an utter end: affliction shall not rise up the second time."

Time stood still. The room suddenly became a haven of hope. I felt the dark cloak over my mind begin to melt away. Tears started streaming down my face. It washed away the word vengeance. Fear became Faith. Weeping became worship. Vengeance became victory.

God had seen me sitting and weeping in Moab. And He had sent a message of hope to me. The affliction would not return the second time. I knew this was from the Lord.

I suddenly realized that little lady was a messenger of God. There was no way that she knew my battle. Only Mike and God knew. And God delivered me and restored my hope.

I sat there weeping, remembering how dead I felt inside and how my life was restored. Tears of hope washed my soul. And now, every time those words forecasting recurrence come to me, I send them to my friend, Nahum. That minor prophet became a major prophet in my life. And I have never been the same.

I am not sure when, but at a certain point it dawned on me—that little lady who gave me the napkin bore a striking resemblance to the one who hugged me in the elevator. That made me shake my head with wonder and utter a long "Hmmm."

And I am still wondering about that.

Hope Scriptures

Psalms 31:24

Be of good courage, and he shall strengthen your heart, all you who hope in the LORD.

Psalms 33:18

Behold, the eye of the Lord is on those who fear Him, on those who hope in His mercy.

Psalms 33:22

Let Your mercy, O Lord, be upon us, just as we hope in You.

Psalms 38:15

For in You, O LORD, I hope; You will hear, O Lord my God.

Psalms 39:7

And now, Lord, what do I wait for? My hope is in You.

Psalms 42:5

Why are you cast down, O my soul? And why are you disquieted within me? Hope in God, for I shall yet praise Him for the help of His countenance.

Jeremiah 31:17

"There is hope in your future," says the Lord, "that your children shall come back to their own border."

Lamentations 3:24

"The Lord is my portion," says my soul, "therefore I hope in Him!"

Psalms 16:8-9

I set the LORD always before me; because He is at my right hand I shall not be moved. Therefore my heart is glad, and my glory rejoices; my flesh also will rest in hope.

Hope Quotes

"We must accept finite disappointment, but never lose infinite hope." —Martin Luther King Jr.

"I dwell in possibility." —Emily Dickinson

"May your choices reflect your hopes, not your fears." —Nelson Mandela

"Most of the important things in the world have been accomplished by people who have kept on trying when there seemed to be no hope at all." —Dale Carnegie

"Where there is no vision, there is no hope." —George Washington Carver

"In all things, it is better to hope than to despair." —Johann Wolfgang von Goethe

"Once you choose hope, anything's possible." —Christopher Reeve

"Optimism is the faith that leads to achievement. Nothing can be done without hope and confidence." —Helen Keller

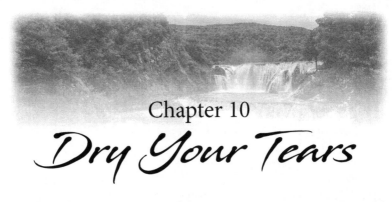

Chapter 10
Dry Your Tears

C harles Dickens said, "We need never be ashamed of our tears, for they are like rain upon the blinding dust of earth." Tears, like raindrops, can soak the fertile soil of a heart inclined toward God and bring forth much fruit in our lives.

Tears can move the very heart of God.

We can take a lesson from Hezekiah. When He was told he would die, he wept bitterly. It was only then that God sent Isaiah the prophet to give him a message, "I've heard your prayer, I have seen your tears; surely, I will heal you" (2 Kings 20:5).

And then, Hezekiah dried his tears.

So, tears can have a purpose.

When Lincoln got the telegram that General Lee was about to surrender, he left Washington to go to the Southern capital of Richmond. He found officials preparing for his entry into that blood-soaked arena of battle. Their plans were to make it a grand celebration. The South had been defeated.

Lincoln immediately rejected the idea. He lamented, "There shall be no triumphal entry into this city of Richmond. There shall be no demonstration of power." He even refused to ride in a carriage. Instead, he walked alone into the city with his head bowed, tears streaming down his face, and his heart heavy with sorrow. He went in and sat at the desk of Jefferson Davis. He put his head in his hands and wept. His sympathetic heart bound the North and South together.

Pride and a gloating smile of victory could have widened the division between the North and South, but a great man's humble tears cemented this split nation and brought it together once again.

Lincoln was just one of the many great men who won great victories with the power of tears. Lincoln dried his tears and the country was made whole again.

So, tears really can have a purpose and they really can give birth to transformation and change.

Three times, the Bible records tears flowing from Jesus' eyes, but then, He dried His tears and did something significant to fulfill His purpose.

At the Grave

In John 11:33-36, Jesus was looking at Mary, who had collapsed in grief in front of him. She claimed, concerning her brother, Lazarus, who had been sick, "Lord, if You had been here, my brother would not have died."

When Jesus saw her weeping, and all those who had come along with her also weeping, he was deeply moved in spirit and troubled. "Where have you laid him?" he asked. "Come and see, Lord," they replied. And then, the shortest verse in the Bible explains:

"Jesus wept."

I believe, it wasn't just the death of his friend that caused the Savior pain; rather, it was also the tears on Mary's face that brought Him to tears. When Jesus saw that look of sorrow and grief in Mary's eyes and on the faces of those who were with her, He was overwhelmed with emotion. He was touched with their pain and He is with ours, too.

The Bible says, "For we do not have a High Priest who cannot sympathize with our weaknesses, but was in all points tempted as we are, yet without sin." (Hebrews 4:15).

Jesus understands our pain. He knows every scar and every surgery. He knows every heartbreak and headache. Sometimes, people wonder where God is when it hurts, when bad things happen, and tragedy strikes. The answer is—He's right there with you—ready to resurrect you, too. Just as He commanded, "Lazarus, come forth!"—He just may be sending forth His command to you also.

At the City

On Palm Sunday, just before Jesus made his triumphant entry into Jerusalem, Luke shares the second recorded time that Jesus cried:

Now as He drew near, He saw the city and wept over it, saying, "If you had known, even you, especially in this your day, the things that make for your peace! But now they are hidden from your eyes. For days will come upon you when your enemies will build an embankment around you, surround you and close you in on every side, and level you, and your children within you, to the ground; and they will not leave in you one stone upon another, because you did not know the time of your visitation" (Luke 19:41-44).

But then, He dried His tears and mounted a donkey to fulfill Zechariah's prophecy ("Rejoice greatly, O daughter of Zion! Shout, O daughter of Jerusalem! Behold, your King is coming to you; He is just and having salvation, Lowly and riding on a donkey, a colt, the foal of a donkey."—Zechariah 9:9)

That was one of the most remarkable moments of Jesus' life—riding into the city on a donkey, crowds gathering around him, worshiping, and throwing their clothing and palm leaves on the ground. Their voices sounded like a heavenly choir, "Blessed is He who comes in the name of the Lord. Hosanna in the highest!"

Jesus was about to be ushered toward the city with a hero's welcome; yet before He rode in, He broke down in passionate sobs. Why? Why did Jesus weep so passionately at the sight of Jerusalem? The answer is simply because He knew that the majority would not accept Him as their Messiah. And because of that, they would suffer serious consequences. So their failure was a grief to Him, knowing He came to save them. Unrequited love is what we call it now.

At the Garden

Shortly afterward, Jesus led his followers to the Garden of Gethsemane. That garden, with its oil press in the center, provided Jesus with a quiet place to spend some of his final hours. It was around midnight. The garden was lit by the night sky and all its stars. Crickets may have been chirping in the background. A garden is supposed to be a peaceful place. But that night, it was not peaceful; it was full of turmoil. That setting would become the stage upon which Jesus' would face his greatest struggle, and he did so with tears. As His sweat mingled with blood, He faced off with death (and the prospect of becoming a sin offering for mankind). He let His tears drive Him to His knees. He earnestly prayed, saying:

"Abba, Father, all things are possible for You. Take this cup away from Me; nevertheless, not what I will, but what You will" (Mark 14:36).

> When we are overwhelmed at what we are facing, tears drive us to place ourselves in the hands of a loving Father.

That is what tears teach us. When we face life's challenges, when we struggle with our own decisions, when we are overwhelmed at what we are facing, tears drive us to place ourselves in the hands of a loving Father. Jesus cried:

Abba, Father (meaning *Dear Father*—a term of deep respect and endearment).

When our faith is tested—we, too, can surrender to God's will and lift our tear-stained face toward heaven crying, "Abba, Father."

The most amazing thing happens then. In a sense, God turns His head and bends His ear to listen to us. Prayer becomes our greatest resource and our greatest power. Tears push us to pray, so they push us to the place of power. Then, even though it was not the answer He wanted, Jesus dried His tears and stood up to fulfill His calling.

There always comes a time when you must decide to stop crying and rise to action. They served their purpose. They pushed you to pray. Now it's time to fulfill your purpose. I know many times, years ago, I would look at my children and say, "Stop the crying. I can't understand you if you are crying." It was my way of saying, "We cannot move on until you dry your tears."

The same is true for us.

I have a favorite scripture concerning the ultimate step from time into eternity that we will all take:

He will wipe away every tear from their eyes, and death shall be no more, neither shall there be mourning, nor crying, nor pain anymore, for the former things have passed away (Revelation 21:4 ESV).

Now this is something to rejoice over. God is going to help us dry our tears. Then we will be able to boldly say:

You have delivered my soul from death, my eyes from tears, and my feet from stumbling; I will walk before the Lord in the land of the living (Psalms 116:8–9).

Yes, that is our destiny—

Weeping may endure for a night, but joy comes in the morning (Psalms 30:5).

Epilogue

Things Cancer Taught Me

Anxiety and Stress Are Not Your Friends.

Have you ever noticed how much people are stressed out? Take a look around you. You see it at the traffic lights, the grocery stores, even in our churches. It seems like almost everyone is stressed, anxious, uptight, and in panic mode. If this is you, stop it right now! Yes, I said, "Stop!" Quote a scripture, think of something positive, go to that happy place in your mind, anything . . . but don't let that emotion control you. You control it. Take the reins: pull back, then hand them to God. Proverbs 25:28 (KJV) says:

> *He that hath no rule over his own spirit is like a city that is broken down, and without walls.*

You don't want to be a broken-down city without walls. There is nothing to restrain the enemy from taking over. Rule your spirit. Sometimes, I still find myself getting worked up in stressful situations. I just don't have the time or patience for it.

One day, Destiny was telling me how very stressful the day had been. As a young teenager, I know her dilemma seemed to be great. I couldn't help but break into a laugh. It was something like someone had not texted her back. With tears rolling down her cheeks, she said, "You have no idea how hard life is?

You don't understand my pain." I looked at her laughing and said, "Cancer, baby, now that is something to cry about." We both laughed. When I do notice my stress levels start to rise, I think to myself, *Is this really that important? Is this a life-or-death situation?* And the answer is always, "No." You have to put things into perspective. And then you snap out of it and move on.

Again, I say, "Rule your spirit!"

Waste No Time Doing Something You Hate.

For too long, Mike and I endured situations that we hated—ministerially. We kept thinking it would get better. Maybe people would make a change in their lives. Maybe wisdom would finally prevail. We wasted precious hours, days, and years trying to make puzzle pieces fit that didn't belong. No more! We don't do that. Illness brings everything into a new perspective. It is amazing how many people fall into the trap of being comfortable in a situation that makes them unhappy—a job, a relationship, a church, a mindset. Whatever it is, if it's making you miserable, get out. Of course, this is not a blanket rule that fits every situation, but if it's keeping you from being your best for the kingdom of God, leave it behind.

> I see things in new ways now, and I value every minute in a deeper measure than many people who have never had a close encounter with death.

Seriously, time is so precious that you don't want to waste a second of it. I see things in new ways now, and I value every minute in a deeper measure than many people who have never had a close encounter with death. I still have times when something strikes me, and I feel tears in my eyes, because I am just so overwhelmed that I am still alive. Being alive is AWESOME. I feel very blessed to be alive, every single day.

So, you choose happiness. Choose you. Wring the best out of every day and every opportunity, like you wring water out of a dish rag. Once you make that choice, good things will start to happen. You will no longer wake up hating the day. You won't be crying because you are stuck in the same old horrible, soul-draining situation.

Choose a good life and choose to value every minute.

Vacation Often.

I was diagnosed with cancer a couple of months before the family was headed to Disney (my Happy Place). Cancelling that trip was so hard. We were going at Christmas. All the reservations were made. The Christmas party was booked. I sat on the bed crying as I told the cast member at Disney Reservations that we weren't going to make it. When she asked me about rebooking, I broke down sobbing. She had no idea. But in my mind, I thought there would never be another trip, never another vacation, or I might never experience happiness again. I know, a bit on the dramatic side. But so true. Rebooking that trip and finally getting to go back to Disney was pure joy. And now, every time I book something new, I look up to heaven and say, "Thank you."

We've travelled a bunch since the beginning of my bout with cancer, little trips here and there, and bigger trips several times a year. We have made memories. We take our vacations. After going through a life-threatening disease that makes travel impossible, you dream about being anywhere but a doctor's office or a treatment ward. You never take going on vacation or quality time with your family for granted again. You enjoy those moments of togetherness.

> Cancer teaches you what is really important. Making memories with those you love is one of the most important things to do.

Cancer teaches you what is really important. Making memories with those you love is one of the most important things to do. Don't wait until it is too late to enjoy this life that God has given you. If He died so you could have life and life more abundantly, then please do "life . . . more abundantly" (John 10:10). Life is a gift. Unwrap that gift and enjoy every minute of it.

Take Care of Your Health.

Yep, this is the big one. And one that I truthfully struggled with. I don't think it's possible to go through something like cancer without having a new appreciation for how amazing your body is when it's working properly. I understand now that when you put the proper fuel in your body, it runs without a hitch. Mike has always been a health person. I would laugh at his eating habits. I would call him a rabbit for eating all those raw carrots. I made fun of his Kombucha drinks; I got a lot of joy making fun of his health nut ways (and I'm talking about raw, organic, unsalted nuts—whew, how many times I've heard the spiel!).

But since cancer showed up in my life, I have taken my health and my diet so much more seriously. I was a junk food addict. Candy bars, chips, and soda were my food pyramid. Salad didn't work for me. Vegetables, are you kidding? Get a hamburger and fries for me. Cancer changed me. Food and I had always had a complex relationship. I had to take control of my tastebuds and retrain my mind to be open to healthy choices. I eliminated sugar from my diet. This was so hard. But I did it (most of the time). This body is a temple. It is God's temple. When we mistreat it, we are mistreating God. That's a tough statement, isn't it?

> This body is a temple. It is God's temple. When we mistreat it, we are mistreating God.

It has been a battle, but I feel so much better. I listen to my body. I listen to my doctors. And I pray a lot about my health. I love the promise of Jeremiah 30:17, "I will restore health unto you and I will heal your wounds." In fact, that's on a plaque in my kitchen.

After my first surgery, the wounds were so profound. I couldn't stand to look at them. I started quoting that scripture continually. My wounds healed quickly. The doctors couldn't believe it. Now when I look at the scars, I don't struggle to accept them. I rejoice in them. They are a reminder of my health and my healing. He has restored my body and my soul. And now, I choose to eat well, exercise, rest, and drink lots of water, pure water. Why? Because I want to live long and good.

Fulfill Your Purpose.

You were created to do something phenomenal with your life. Maybe you have been waiting for the right moment. The moment is now. Time is not stopping. You are destined for greatness. Everything we go through is a lesson learned that we can then teach others.

What is your purpose? What is your destiny? The whole time I was going through my journey, I kept thinking . . . I didn't do this . . . I wish I had done that. It was a constant thought running through my brain. I wish, I want, I would have, O, if I had just been more bold in my faith!

Words need actions. So now, after cancer, my daily morning thought is, *What am I meant to do today? What is my purpose?* And I go for it.

There is no better time to start fulfilling your calling than now. You don't have to wait for a tragedy to bring it on. Dive in, with all your might. Don't be afraid of failure. When you are at the end of your life, you want to be able to look back over your years with a smile and say, "I did that! I tried that! I didn't give up! You want to be able to say, "I not only made lemonade out of those lemons, I used all the zest from the peel!!!"

So, there you have it, I lived. I have told my story. It may be different from your story. But that is the beauty of life. Differences make us unique and uniqueness should make us appreciate each other more.

I pray you live a life full of adventure and excitement.

And may I remind you once again—Live Abundantly!!!

Elizabeth Shreve has traveled for years sharing her heart and the beauty of the Gospel, in churches, women's meetings, conferences, and with many individuals (who are just as important as the large gatherings).

If you would like to invite her for a speaking engagement, you may contact her one of the following ways:

Office phone: 423-478-2843
Personal email address: Elizshreve@gmail.com
The "Contact" page on our website:
www.shreveministries.org

Multiple copies of this book are available at a discounted price. For information, call our office or email us: info@shreveministries.org.

www.facebook.com/shreveministries
www.YouTube.com/mikeshreveministries

---

1. The song "Here I Am to Worship" is Copyright © 2001 Thankyou Music (PRS) (adm. worldwide at CapitolCMGPublishing.com excluding the UK & Europe which is adm. atIntegratedRights.com) All rights reserved. Used by permission.